THE
LONDON & BIRMINGHAM
RAILWAY
THROUGH HARROW
1837 – 1987

Laurence Menear's meticulous line drawing of Harrow & Wealdstone Station from his book London's Underground Stations — A Social and Architectural Study *(Midas Books, 1983).*

Laurence Menear.

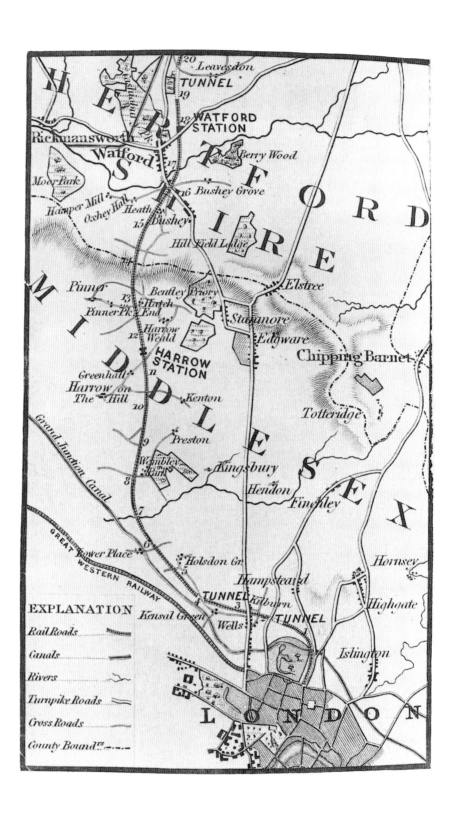

Frontispiece map from Francis Coghlan's Iron Road Book and Railway Companion from London to Birmingham, Manchester, and Liverpool *(published in 1838) shewing the line from London to Watford. Harrow Parish, with Pinner Parish, extended from the River Brent at mile 7 to the county boundary at mile 14. Note that Greenhill erroneously appears as "Greenhall", and Harlesden (Green) and Cassiobury Park do not have their present-day spellings.*

Courtesy Hertfordshire Library Service, Watford Libraries.

PETER G. SCOTT

Eng. Tech, AMI Elec IE.

THE
LONDON & BIRMINGHAM
RAILWAY
THROUGH HARROW

1837–1987

A celebration of 150 years of the Euston Main Line through the London Borough of Harrow.

The journey begins. The Royal Scot *train hauled by the locomotive of the same name (LMS 4-6-0 No. 6100) prepares to leave Euston to the accompaniment of Scottish pipers. The occasion is the commencement of the full summer services on 18th. July, 1932.*

B.B.C. Hulton Picture Library.

The design of the Borough Arms, of which this is a facsimile of reduced size, is that shewn upon the Grant of Arms, dated May 3rd, 1938, and the Grant of Supporters to the Arms, dated September 10th, 1954. It has also been used by the London Borough of Harrow since its formation in 1965.

DESCRIPTION OF ARMS
BLAZON
EXTRACTED FROM THE GRANT OF ARMS
dated May 3rd, 1938, to the Harrow Urban District Council.

Or a Fesse arched Vert in chief on a Pile Gules between a Torche Sable enflamed proper and a Quill pen of the fourth a Clarion of the first and in a base upon a Mount issuant a Hurst of Trees of the Second And for the Crest Issuant from a Mural Crown proper a demi Lion holding between the paws An Arrow fessewise Argent enfiled with a Wreath of Oak also proper.

EXTRACTED FROM THE
GRANT OF SUPPORTERS TO THE ARMS
dated September 10th, 1954

On the dexter side a representation of Hygeia supporting with her exterior hand a Staff entwined with a Snake and on the sinister side a Benedictine Monk, supporting with his exterior hand a Staff all proper. Hygeia, the Goddess of Health, typifies the excellent health record of the Borough. The Benedictine Monk recalls the long association of the Borough with the Church through the Archbishops of Canterbury, the ancient Priory of Bentley Priory and in other directions.

The design exemplifies the whole Borough, the allusions being as follows:

The shield is centrally broken by a broad horizontal green band, indicating the large proportion of open spaces in the Borough, and the interest of the area in the Green Belt; in the upper half of the shield appear (1) the torch of knowledge to the left, (2) a quill, which represents, heraldically, the Pinner area and the eminent writers who have been associated with the Borough, to the right, and (3) in the centre, a 'pile' representing in shape the Gore in which were held the meetings of the Saxon Moot of the old Saxon parish of Harrow and referring also to the present petty sessional division; the 'pile' was also a feature of the arms of the Chandos family; in the centre of the 'pile' is an organ rest, which alludes to the connexion of Handel with the Borough. In the lower half of the shield appears a clump of trees representing the Wealdstone and Harrow Weald areas which, until comparatively recently, were part of the great Weald of Middlesex; the clump of trees stand on a mound typifying the Hill of Harrow on the Hill. The shield is surmounted by the conventional mural crown with the heraldic figure of a lion holding a laurel wreath through which is a silver arrow; the lion, laurel wreath and the arrow appearing also in the arms of Harrow School.

The motto on the scroll is "Salus populi suprema lex", which may be translated as "The well-being of the people is the highest law".

This is the eleventh work produced at the request of the panel for Local History Publications and issued under the imprint of the London Borough of Harrow. The Panel was set up in 1977 at the suggestion of the Harrow Development Council for Adult Education, in order to encourage the study of local history, by recommending suitable works for publication to the Borough's Leisure Committee. The membership of the Panel is as follows: *Chairman:* Councillor Owen Cock. *Members:* Councillors A. Hamlin, P. Harrison, and M.G. Nutt; Mrs C. Baker, Miss H. Shorter, Miss H. Wigmore, and Messrs. A.W. Ball, A. Dark, C. Gee, J. Mann, B. Mathur, and P.G. Scott.

"The London & Birmingham Railway Through Harrow" first published 1987.

International Standard Book Number 0 901034 10 X (hardback)   0 901034 11 8 (paperback)

Designed by "Hartest Productions", Greenhill, Middlesex.

Published by the London Borough of Harrow, Civic Centre, Station Road, Wealdstone, Harrow, Middlesex.

Printed in Great Britain by the Kingswood Press, 9 Palmerston Road, Wealdstone, Harrow, Middlesex.

Contents

"The station staff knew which trains the various passengers caught, and if a
passenger was late and the train was not held up for him there was trouble." —
Station Foreman Charles D. Cawley recalling his early days at Harrow &
Wealdstone. (Harrow Observer & Gazette, 28th. August, 1952.)

Station staff, cab drivers and omnibus
staff at Harrow & Wealdstone Station
early this century.
Courtesy G.H.C. Champniss.

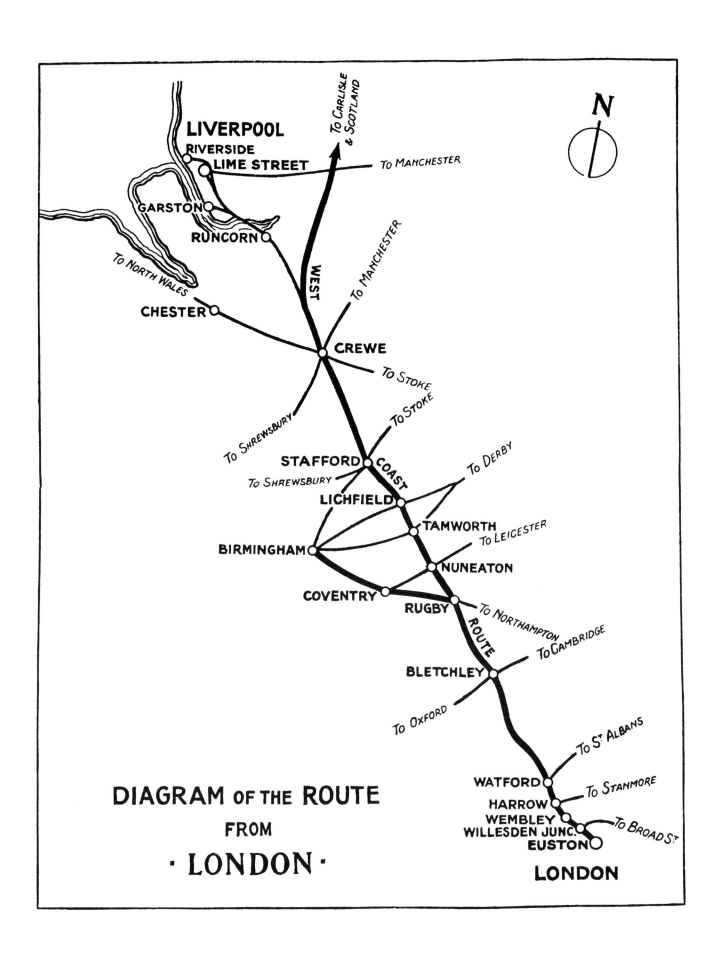

N

LIVERPOOL
RIVERSIDE
LIME STREET
To Manchester
To Carlisle & Scotland
GARSTON
RUNCORN
To North Wales
WEST
To Manchester
CHESTER
CREWE
To Stoke
To Shrewsbury
To Stoke
COAST
To Derby
STAFFORD
To Shrewsbury
LICHFIELD
TAMWORTH
To Leicester
BIRMINGHAM
NUNEATON
COVENTRY
RUGBY
To Northampton
To Cambridge
ROUTE
BLETCHLEY
To Oxford
To St Albans
WATFORD
To Stanmore
HARROW
WEMBLEY
To Broad St
WILLESDEN JUNC.
EUSTON
LONDON

DIAGRAM OF THE ROUTE
FROM
· LONDON ·

The London & Birmingham and West Coast routes from London Euston, adapted from the map in LMS Route Book No. 2.
Courtesy British Rail, London Midland Region.

PREFACE

It is now difficult to imagine the rural Middlesex of 150 years ago. The Harrow Road and the Edgware Road were country lanes, and Hyde Park and Regent's Park were on the outskirts of built-up London. The journey by stage coach from Harrow to London would have taken the best part of half a day, but we now complete this distance in just fifteen minutes, thanks to the London & Birmingham Railway. Railways soon gained great popularity in those early years, and at the height of the 'railway mania' there were lines promoted from everywhere to anywhere. Sadly, things have never been quite the same since the Second World War, and with Dr. Beeching's infamous report — *The Reshaping of British Railways* — went the majority of the branch lines. However, the London & Birmingham route from Euston is the London Midland Region's busiest main line, and its electrification doubled the railway passenger journeys between London and the North-West.

Harrow's other 'main line', the Metropolitan, has been the subject of at least four books in recent years. This is probably due to the fact that the 'Met' is now only a shadow of its former self, evoking memories of days gone by when it was in its prime. In comparison with the Metropolitan, the London & Birmingham line has been somewhat neglected in print recently. It was with some apprehension that I suggested the idea of this book to the Panel for Local History Publications, thinking that it might be difficult to find enough information specifically relating to the Harrow area. I'm glad to say that I was wrong. After a year's extensive research this is the result, and I hope it adequately fills a gap in local railway history. It was most gratifying to locate two 1837 views drawn at the original Harrow Station; one was found in Camden at the beginning of the line, and the other in Birmingham at the end.

I would like to place on record my thanks to the many individuals and institutions that have helped in compiling this history. The railway organizations and staff have been most co-operative, and I give my grateful thanks to the following: The Public Affairs Department of British Rail, London Midland Region, at Stanier House, Birmingham, and the Area Manager's Office at Watford Junction; Mr. Mike Champion, Assistant Station Manager at Willesden; Mr. John Bingham, Chargeman at Harrow & Wealdstone, and the staff at Kenton, Harrow & Wealdstone, Headstone Lane, and Hatch End stations; Mr. Charles F. Cawley (who started his railway career as a Junior Porter at Harrow & Wealdstone and completed 48 years' service, — his father was Station Foreman at Harrow from 1911 to 1952); Mr. Donald G. Evans (formerly Station Master at Kenton); Mr. Bill Merritt (Guard of the 7.31 a.m. Tring-Euston train on 8th. October, 1952); The Railway Technical Centre at Derby; London Regional Transport; The London & North Western Railway Society; and The Locomotive Club of Great Britian.

The following Local History Librarians are thanked for their valuable assistance: Mr. Bob Thomson at the Civic Centre Library, Wealdstone (London Borough of Harrow); Mr. David Johnson at the Watford Public Library (Hertfordshire Library Service); and Mr. Malcolm Holmes at the Swiss Cottage Library (London Borough of Camden). The staff of the following libraries, record offices, and museums, are also thanked for their help: Civic Centre Library, Wealdstone; Public Record Office, Kew; Greater London Record Office and History Library, Clerkenwell; British Library, Bloomsbury; British Library Newspaper Library, Colindale; Ironbridge Gorge Museum, Telford; National Railway Museum, York; and the B.B.C. Hulton Picture Library, Saint Marylebone.

My sincere thanks are also due to Julia Elton, Mrs. M. Forsyth, Reverend Bruce Kinsey, Messrs. John Barnacle, Ian Brown, Dilwyn Chambers, G.H.C. Champniss, Lewis Coles, L.F.E. Coombs, John Cummings, Jim Golland, George McGechan, Geoffrey Kichenside, Laurence Menear, Alf Porter, and John Stanaway; and also to Ian Allan, *The Architectural Review*, Central Press Photos, David & Charles, *The Harrow Observer & Gazette*, Harrow Post Office, Her Majesty's Stationery Office, Higgs & Hill, The Kingswood Press, Oxford Publishing Company, *The Railway Gazette*, Watney Combe Reid & Company, George Wells Photographic Services, and A. Wooster & Sons. Thanks to Peter and Stella Walker for the typing, Councillor Dick Hains for his interest, and the Panel for Local History Publications for their encouragement. My apologies to anybody I have inadvertently missed out.

Greenhill, Middlesex.   Peter G. Scott.
May, 1987.

MILEPOSTS

Some Early Mileposts in British Railway History

1803   July. 26th.   Surrey Iron Railway opens — world's first public railway; goods only, horse traction.

1804   Feb. 21st.   First locomotive to run on rails; built by Trevithick (Pen-y-darran Tramroad, South Wales).

1807   March 25th.   Oystermouth Railway opens — world's first public passenger railway; horse traction.

1808   July-Sept.   Trevithick's locomotive *Catch-me-who-can* exhibited on a circular track by the New Road (Euston Road) in Saint Pancras

1825   Sept. 27th.   Stockton & Darlington Railway opens — first *public* railway to use locomotives (built by George Stephenson) but for goods only; passenger trains still hauled by horses

1829   Oct. 6th-14th   "Rainhill Locomotive Trials" on Liverpool & Manchester Railway won by *Rocket* built by George and Robert Stephenson.

1830   Sept. 15th.   Liverpool & Manchester Railway opens — first public railway with all traffic operated by steam.

1836   Feb.8th.   London & Greenwich Railway opens — first public railway in London.

1837   July 20th.   *LONDON & BIRMINGHAM RAILWAY* opens from Euston to Box Moor — *FIRST MAIN LINE FROM LONDON.*

1838   June 4th.   Great Western Railway opens from Paddington to Maidenhead.

The Great Western Railway celebrated its 150th. anniversary in 1985, which was not strictly correct; the GWR always commemorated the date of its Act of Parliament instead of its date of opening.

TIME TABLE FOR JUNE, 1858.

LONDON AND NORTH WESTERN RAILWAY.—To and from London, Harrow, Watford, St. Albans, &c.

William Winkley Jun. was the printer and publisher of the Harrow Gazette, *and he regularly printed the train times in his newspaper, as illustrated above. He also produced the 'HARROW POCKET RAILWAY TIME TABLE'...*
"At the repeated request of several of W. WINKLEY'S customers, he has been induced to publish the Time Table on a small folding card, suitable for the waistcoat pocket." (Harrow Gazette & General Advertiser, 1st. June, 1858.)
Harrow Local History Collection, London Borough of Harrow.

INTRODUCTION

Nineteen-hundred and eighty-seven is an important year in the history of railways through the London Borough of Harrow. On 20th. July the first section of the London & Birmingham Railway (the Euston Main Line) celebrates its 150th. anniversary. Harrow & Wealdstone Station is also 150 years old on this date, although no part of the original station survives. By coincidence, this year also sees the 75th. anniversary of the opening of the D.C. electric 'New Line' to Harrow & Wealdstone, the 60th. anniversary of the *Royal Scot* train, and the 21st. anniversary of the main line a.c. electrification from Euston.

This book takes a look at the history of Robert Stephenson's pioneer London & Birmingham Railway through the Borough of Harrow. Particular emphasis is given to Harrow Station (the 'Wealdstone' suffix was not added until 1897) as it was the first station to be built in the Parish of Harrow (the fore-runner of the present Borough). Harrow Parish originally included Wembley, so a description of the line through this area is also included.

In 1846 the London & Birmingham became part of the new London & North Western Railway (abbreviated to 'LNWR' or 'North Western'), which was described as the "largest joint-stock corporation in the world". On the back of its official picture postcards the North Western proudly proclaimed that it was "...noted for Punctuality, Speed, Smooth Riding, Dustless Tracks, Safety and Comfort, and is the Oldest Established Firm in the Railway Passenger Business". The last part of this statement is always open to dispute; the North Western's claim was obviously based on the fact that one of its constituents, the Liverpool & Manchester, was the first railway to operate all public services by steam, but the Oystermouth Railway (latterly called the Swansea & Mumbles Railway) was the first actual public passenger railway.

The London & North Western was the self-styled 'Premier Line', and its excellent main line services certainly lived up to this title. There were occasional attempts to apply the 'Premier' name to the Great Western Railway, but to do so, as C. Hamilton Ellis* so succinctly put it, "was in as bad taste as to introduce religious or political controversy to the conversation at one of the vicar's tea parties".

Local personalities associated with the railway were George Findlay (later Sir George), General Manager of the LNWR (1880-1893) who lived at Hill House, Edgware, and is buried at Little Stanmore; and George Carr Glyn, who lived at Stanmore Park and was Chairman of both the London & Birmingham (1837 - 1846) and the London & North Western (1846 - 1852). *The Times** noted that "Mr. Glyn, who was created Lord Wolverton in 1869, looked upon railway enterprise with the eye of a statesman, and saw in the great invention of George Stephenson the means of extending civilization, commerce, and enlightenment such as the world had never previously possessed". The pulpit at Great Stanmore parish church was given in his memory.

The Harrow & Stanmore Railway, the first branch line in the Harrow area, also receives attention in this book. The line was promoted by Frederick Gordon of Bentley Priory, who was much loved and respected in the district. Another local personality was the Reverend J.W. Cunningham, Vicar of Harrow, who took a great interest in everything, not least the railway. His name often appears in the London & Birmingham's minute books, as we shall see in the following pages.

The London & Birmingham (and the North Western to a lesser extent) had separate committees for just about everything imaginable. They included the 'Coaching and Police Committee' (signalmen were originally called policemen); the delightful 'Church and Schools Committee', which also operated a lending library along the line for the benefit of staff; the 'London Committee', which deliberated on the London end of the line; and the inevitable 'Committee of Management'. Extensive use has been made of the early minute books of various committees in compiling this history.

In 1923 the LNWR became part of the London Midland & Scottish Railway (LMS), the largest of the 'Big Four' grouped railways. In 1938 the LMS celebrated the centenary of the opening of the London & Birmingham Railway throughout from Euston to Birmingham, and likewise in 1988 British Rail will celebrate the sesquicentenary. At Harrow, being on the first section of line to open, the anniversary is marked the year before, and this modest volume is by way of that celebration.

* See Bibliography

Principal Amalgamations of the Main Line Railway Companies associated with this book

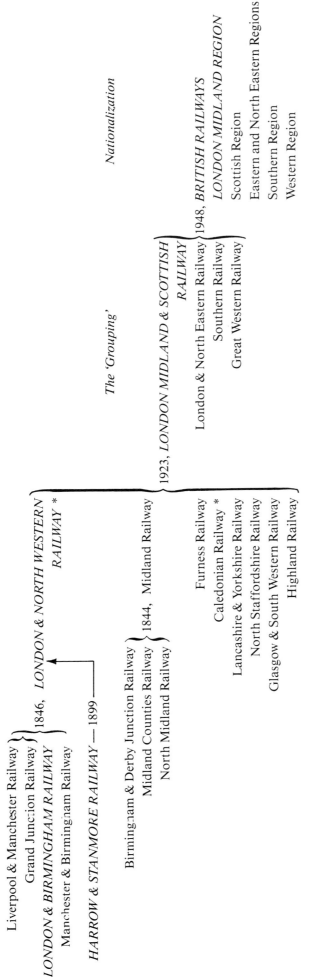

Liverpool & Manchester Railway
Grand Junction Railway
} 1846, *LONDON & NORTH WESTERN RAILWAY* *
LONDON & BIRMINGHAM RAILWAY
Manchester & Birmingham Railway

HARROW & STANMORE RAILWAY — 1899

Birmingham & Derby Junction Railway
Midland Counties Railway
North Midland Railway
} 1844, Midland Railway

Furness Railway
Caledonian Railway *
Lancashire & Yorkshire Railway
North Staffordshire Railway
Glasgow & South Western Railway
Highland Railway

The 'Grouping'

} 1923, *LONDON MIDLAND & SCOTTISH RAILWAY*

London & North Eastern Railway
Southern Railway
Great Western Railway
} 1948, *BRITISH RAILWAYS*

Nationalization

LONDON MIDLAND REGION
Scottish Region
Eastern and North Eastern Regions
Southern Region
Western Region

* These two companies operated the '*West Coast Route*' from London to Scotland. (The name is somewhat a misnomer as the line is only within sight of the sea for a short distance north of Lancaster.)

The LNWR adopted Britannia as its emblem, and there are an almost uncountable number of different versions. Britannia can look like a youthful young woman or resemble a tight-lipped Queen Victoria, the train on the viaduct (which has a variable number of arches) can be running in either direction, and the lion's expression ranges from a friendly station moggy's 'come and stroke me' to an M-G-M growl. By contrast, the LMS device is rather uninteresting, consisting of a dragon's wing charged with a red cross (the City of London's crest) which previously appeared atop the London & Birmingham's shield, and roses and thistles to denote England and Scotland. The BR crest illustrated shews a demi-lion rampant (definitely growling this time) holding a wheel; and a crown decorated with a rose, a thistle, an oak leaf and two Welsh leeks. BR also used the 'hot dog' totem, most notably on station signs, but from 1965 a new symbol has been used, consisting of "two-way traffic arrows on parallel lines representing tracks". Rule Britannia!

The familiar bar and circle symbol of the Underground Group appeared outside LMS New Line stations served by the Bakerloo Line.

Illustrations from Peter G. Scott's collection, except where stated.

The London & Birmingham Railway Company's armorial device consisted of the arms of the cities in its name, London on the left and Birmingham on the right.
Courtesy National Railway Museum, York.

The Harrow & Stanmore Railway used Frederick Gordon's boars' heads device surrounded with thistles and roses.

Notes for the assistance of the reader

Measurements

Railways are traditionally measured in miles and chains, and areas in acres, roods and perches. The Imperial measurements found in this book are as follows:

Linear

12 inches =	1 foot	
	3 feet =	1 yard
1 perch, rod or pole =	16½ feet =	5½ yards
4 perches =	66 feet =	22 yards =	1 chain
10 chains =	660 feet =	220 yards =	1 furlong
80 chains or 8 furlongs =	5280 feet =	1760 yards =	1 mile.

Area

1 (square) perch, rod or pole	=	30¼ square yards	
40 (square) perches	=	1210 square yards	= 1 rood
4 roods	=	4840 square yards	= 1 acre.

Money

Until 1971 the pound sterling (£) was divided into 20 shillings (s.) or 240 pence (d.):

12d. = 1s. (or 1/-)

20s. (or 20/-) = £1 (also written as 1*l.* in the 19th century).

Spellings

Original spellings are used in the quotations from old documents and minute books. The 'long s' is represented by the character '*f*'.

Directions

The London & Birmingham Railway through Harrow runs in the general direction of south-east to north-west. For ease of reference, however, it is regarded in this book as running from south to north.

In common with standard British railway practice, 'Up' trains run on the 'Up' line *towards* London, and 'Down' trains run on the 'Down' line *away* from London.

The London & Birmingham Railway originally followed the coaching practice of issuing hand written way-bills as the passengers' authority to travel. Thomas Edmondson, a station clerk on the Newcastle & Carlisle Railway, soon devised a simple system based on cardboard tickets, which the London & Birmingham introduced from 1841. Two Edmondson-type tickets are illustrated below:

Tickets from Peter G. Scott's collection.

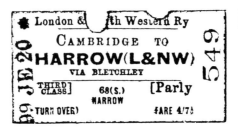

An LNWR 3rd. class Parliamentary single issued in 1899. Gladstone's Parliament laid down that there must be a daily service at not more than a penny a mile over every line. On the reverse of this ticket, in the tiniest of printing, is a lengthy 'conditions of issue' notice which records that the ticket is not available by the Irish Mail.

(Ticket colour-dark green.)

An LMS platform ticket issued at Harrow & Wealdstone No. 1 booking office on the Wealdstone side of the station. The No. 2 booking office is on the Greenhill side.

(Ticket colour-white.)

Postscript: *A new computerized ticket issuing system was introduced at Harrow & Wealdstone in March, 1987.*

1 BUILDING THE LINE THROUGH HARROW

"The London and Birmingham Railway was engineered by Robert Stephenson which is a guarantee that it was well planned ... the whole line was laid out with the object of keeping the gradients down to the minimum and thus easing the task of the locomotives..."

From *A Century of Progress, London — Birmingham 1838-1938* (London Midland & Scottish Railway, 1938).

A company was first formed in 1823 with the object of building a railway between London and Birmingham. In January, 1824, Sir John Rennie was asked to survey a route, and levels were taken over a wide area. A report dated 1st. April, 1826, recommended a terminus at Islington alongside the Regent's Canal, and a route to Birmingham *via* (or near) Harrow Weald, Rickmansworth, Watford, Hemel Hempstead, Cheddington, Quainton, Brackley, Southam, and Coventry.

Nothing became of this proposal, but in 1829 two further routes were suggested: one *via* Oxford and Banbury, and the other (by Francis Giles) *via* Coventry. Separate companies were formed to promote each route, but on 11th. September, 1830, they amalgamated to form one united company.

On 15th. September, 1830, the Liverpool & Manchester Railway was opened, and George Findlay, writing later in his book *The Working and Management of an English Railway* (see bibliography) commented on the effect that this line had:

"The great success of the Liverpool and Manchester railway, as might naturally have been expected, let loose a flood of railway enterprise all over the country. Lines were soon projected between all the towns of any importance in the kingdom, and even between remote villages. One enthusiast went so far as to propose a railway under the sea between Dover and Calais, and was no doubt looked upon by his contemporaries as a fitting candidate for a lunatic asylum ... The most important result that immediately followed, however, was the revival of the scheme which had previously been mooted, but had been abandoned, for the construction of a railway between London and Birmingham."

George Stephenson, Engineer of the Liverpool & Manchester Railway, was consulted about the London & Birmingham scheme, and he favoured the route via Coventry. This route was adopted by the promoters, and shortly afterwards George Stephenson and his son Robert were appointed Joint Engineers. In October, 1830, they recommended a terminus near the Edgware Road and Hyde Park, and an exit from London *via* Watford and Hemel Hempstead, instead of Giles's suggestion of Islington as a terminus with a line running *via* Chipping Barnet and South Mimms to Hemel Hempstead.

Another survey was made in 1831 and resulted in the selection of Euston as the London terminus. It was still not evident at this time whether the line would pass to the east or west of Harrow Hill. Further investigation, however, revealed that the line would have to pass to the east of Watford, in a mile-long tunnel, in order to avoid Cassiobury Park and Grove Park (the landowners, the Earls of Essex and Clarendon, were strongly against the railway), and it was also desirable to reduce the amount of earthworks necessary in crossing the Oxhey Ridge on the Middlesex/Hertfordshire boundary. The best route, therefore, from an engineering point of view, was to the east of Harrow Hill. Even so, a short tunnel was thought to be necessary at Oxhey Lane. A Bill embodying the Stephensons' plans was deposited, and read in Parliament for the first time on 20th. February, 1832. The second reading was secured on 28th. February on a division with 146 for and 125 against.

Middlesex was a hay farming area; the heavy clay land produced hay which was considered the best in the country. The farmers were concerned that once the railway arrived, the horse would be doomed, and there would be no market for their hay. The London & Birmingham Railway would undoubtably displace many hundreds of coaching and canal horses, but

what was not realized at the time was that the railways themselves would become the greatest employers of horses, particularly for the collection and delivery of goods and for shunting in yards.* The farmers' fears were unfounded.

While the Bill was in the Commons, Lord Northwick, Lord of the Manor of Harrow and a Governor of Harrow School, withdrew his opposition to it. By way of settlement he at first wanted the railway to construct a new length of road beside the line, but he later settled for some of the Company's shares instead. The Bill was passed by the House of Commons on 19th. June, 1832, but there were still a number of landowners who had not been won over. Consequently, on 10th. July the Bill failed in the House of Lords. George Findlay (*ibidem*) wrote:

"The opposition to this Bill was as unscrupulous, and of precisely the same character, as that which its precursor — the Bill for the Liverpool and Manchester Railway — had had to encounter."

Some of the arguments put up against the Liverpool & Manchester Railway are mentioned by George Findlay. They make amusing reading today:

"...the smoke of the engines would kill the birds, cattle would be terrified, and cows would cease to give their milk; the sparks from the engines would set fire to the houses and manufactories on the line of route; the race of horses would become extinct, and many other direful consequences would ensue, amidst which the absolute ruin of the country would shrink to the insignificance of a detail!"

By the following year the Company had won the approval of more of the landowners (sometimes by paying them treble the value of their land) and a

The statue of George Stephenson (left) in the Great Hall of the old Euston Station, and (right) the statue of Robert Stephenson in Euston Grove, photographed in 1953.
British Rail, London Midland Region.

* As late as 1949 British Railways still employed over 7,000 horses.

further Bill was presented to Parliament. In this Bill the terminus was to be at Camden Town instead of Euston. The Bill progressed successfully through the Commons and the Lords and received the Royal Assent on 6th. May, 1833. The London & Birmingham Railway Company was in business at last.

On 7th. September, 1833, Robert Stephenson was appointed sole engineer, with the approval of his father. Robert was now responsible for the whole of the construction work for a salary of £1,500 per annum, plus £200 for expenses. It is said that when surveying the line he walked from London to Birmingham more than twenty times. On 15th. January, 1834, it was reported to the London & Birmingham's London Committee that the line from London to Ashton (57 miles) had been staked out, and from London to Hatch End the levels and sections had been completed. It was not until the following month, however, that the Committee agreed to secure possession of the land required for the first 20 miles from London. Even before compensation for the owners and lessees had been considered, the contract for building the line through Harrow was let.

The successful bidders for the No.2 (Harrow) Contract were Joseph Nowell and Sons, who agreed to construct the railway from the River Brent to near the River Colne at Watford for the sum of £110,270 7s. 0d. The length of this contract was 9 miles 44 chains. The original contract document survives, and the first of its 69 pages reads as follows (punctuation is largely left to the reader):

> *This Indenture* made the twenty first day of May in the year of our Lord one thousand eight hundred and thirty four *Between The London and Birmingham Railway Company* established and incorporated by an Act of Parliament passed in the third year of the reign of His present Majesty King William the Fourth intituled "An Act for making a Railway from London to Birmingham" of the one part and *Joseph Nowell, John Willans Nowell,* and *Jonathan Willans Nowell* of Leeds in the County of York Contractors of the other part. *Whereas* The London and Birmingham Railway Company have pursuant to the powers and authorities given to them by the above mentioned Act of Parliament determined to make a Railway with the proper works and conveniences connected therewith in the Line or course and upon acrofs under or over the Lands delineated in the plan and described in the Book of Reference deposited with the respective Clerks of the peace for the Counties of Middlesex, Hertford, Buckingham, Northampton, Warwick and Worcester, the Liberty of St. Albans, and the City of Coventry mentioned in and referred to by the said Act that is to say commencing on the West side of the High Road leading from London to Hampstead at or near to the first Bridge Westward of the lock on the Regent's Canal at Camden Town in the Parish of Saint Pancras in the County of Middlesex and terminating at or near to certain gardens called Nova Scotia gardens in the parishes of Ashton Juxta Birmingham and Saint Martin Birmingham in the County of Warwick *And whereas Robert Stephenson, Esquire,* the principle Engineer appointed by the said Company for the purpose of designing and superintending the making of the said Railway and other Works has prepared Plans Sections Drawings and Specifications of the various Works to be done for making and completing a portion of the said intended Railway commencing at the River Brent near Wembley Green in the County of Middlesex and terminating at the South End of the Bridge over the ~~Turnpike~~ Road from Watford to Bushey Heath near the River Colne in the County of Hertford...

Robert Stephenson personally supervised the first nine miles from Camden Town, and divided the remainder of the line into four districts under assistant engineers. About 20 contractors were involved, but some later went bankrupt and Stephenson had to complete the work himself. The first sod was cut at Chalk Farm on 1st. June, 1834.

BUILDING THE LINE THROUGH HARROW

One of Edward Bury's 2-2-0 locomotives supplied to the London & Birmingham Railway. It was not until 1845 that Bury began to build six-wheeled engines which were more stable on the track.
Courtesy Railway Gazette.

In order to appease landowners who were hostile to the railway, or who did not want to keep odd corners of land that were cut-off by the line, the London & Birmingham had to purchase far more land than it actually wanted. A survey of the line completed in 1840 (see Bibliography) gives the following statistics for the Harrow area:

		Acres	roods	perches
Harrow Parish:	Land occupied by line	66.	2.	11.
	Land adjoining	80.	2.	13.
Pinner in Harrow:	Land occupied by line	17.	3.	39.
	Land adjoining	42.	2.	16.

The London & Birmingham therefore had over 123 acres of land in Harrow which it did not require for operating the railway. Most of this surplus land was subsequently leased or sold, but ironically the LNWR had to repurchase some strips of land when the number of tracks along the line was increased: first to three, then to four, and later to six when the electric 'New Line' was built to Watford. A small section of the 1840 survey shewing the Hatch End Farm/Pinner Park area is reproduced on pages 18 and 19, and provides a good example of how much land the railway company had to purchase in order to get the line through; all the cross-hatched areas, plus Maysfield Meadow, were bought by the London & Birmingham.

It was on 21st. May, 1834, that the London Committee considered the purchase of Hatch End Farm:

"Mr Benjamin Weall's estate at Hatch End proposed to be taken by the London & Birmingham Railway Company consists of a respectable farm house, extensive outbuildings, yards and gardens, also six cottage tenements and sundry parcels of Meadow and arable land containing altogether 75 acres 0 roods 23 perches of which 37 acres 2 roods 26 perches is freehold and 37 acres 1 rood 37 perches copyhold — the buildings are freehold.."

It appeared to the Committee that "...it is in the power of Mr. Benjamin Weall, should he be disposed to act hostilely, greatly to retard the possession by the Company of land which is immediately required for the Works of Contract No.2". On the 11th. June, therefore, the London Committee approved a settlement of £8,675, although the farm had been valued at £7,916. The railway company then approached Weall to see if he would be prepared to rent the farm back, less the 4 acres 1 rood 30 perches required for the line. He was only prepared to pay £120 per annum, so on 1st. October, 1834, the London Committee approved the railway's contractors, Joseph Nowell & Sons, as tenants on the following terms:

"Houses, outbuildings, two cottages adjoining at £70 per annum. 59 acres 1 rood 29 perches of land le*f*s the quantity required for the railway, two years certain @ 50/- per acre."

The Nowells used the farm as their base while working on the No.2 (Harrow) Contract. The arable part of the farm not taken by the Nowells was leased by Francis Dancer on a yearly tenancy at 20/- per acre. Most of Hatch End Farm was eventually sold by the LNWR in 1852 and 1857 to the Trustees of the Commercial Travellers' Orphan School.

Next to Hatch End Farm the railway crossed a corner of the Pinner Park Estate, then owned by Saint Thomas's Hospital (and shewn as such on the 1840 survey, *q.v.*). The line occupied just 1 acre 3 roods 10 perches of the Estate, and on 5th. November, 1834, the London Committee approved payment of £492 7s. 0d. to the Hospital and £249 7s. 0d. to Mr. Walkden the tenant. On the east side of the railway a small strip of Saint Thomas's Hospital land was left isolated, but in this instance the land owner did not want to part with it. On 4th. October, 1837, the London Committee instructed their solicitor to negotiate with Saint Thomas's Hospital for an exchange of the portion of their land intersected by the railway for an equal quantity of the Company's land adjoining the Hospital Estate "...to obviate

BUILDING THE LINE THROUGH HARROW

the neceſsity of maintaining a gate and building a lodge at the Pinner Park Croſsing". The Hospital would not give way, however, and the London & Birmingham had to provide a level crossing and built two cottages beside it. In November, 1841, it is recorded that the Estate Committee agreed to charge the policeman at 'Pinner Gates' the sum of £6 10s. 0d. per annum rent on his cottage — he had previously been living there rent free — but at the same time the police working hours were reduced from twelve to eight per day.

Back to 1834, and the London Committee is still agreeing compensation payments to landowners and tenants. Some examples of the payments made in the Harrow area are given below:

An 1837 view looking south from the Oxhey Lane cutting. The spire of Harrow Parish Church can just be seen through the centre arch of the Oxhey Lane Bridge. In the background (below the spire) is the Dove House Bridge.
Harrow Local History Collection, London Borough of Harrow.

	£.	s.	d.
Dean & Chapter of Christ Church, Freehold in the Parish of Harrow 23 acres 2 roods 26 perches	1,361	5	0
Henry Young, Lessee of the same	1,809	9	0
Henry Young's Freehold in the same parish, 17 acres 8 roods (*sic*) (including £57 14s. 3d. for timber and £50 expenses).	2,154	1	9
Mr. George Drummond, Half an acre	70	5	0
John Priest, 2 roods 10 perches land — orchard	130	0	0
Compensation — Buildings, fruit trees &c	760	0	0
Revd. J.W. Cunningham, Parish of Harrow, 32 acres 2 roods 7 perches land	210	0	0
Compensation	65	0	0
Joseph Greenhill, compensation	29	2	0
Lord Northwick, 17 acres 1 rood 37 perches land	3,600	0	0

At the Committee's 11th. June and 18th. June, 1834, meetings it was agreed that Lord Northwick should be given twenty shares in the Company for his Manorial Rights over the land required in the Harrow and Pinner parishes. He was also grossly overpaid for his 17¼ acres of land. The Reverend Cunningham, for nearly twice as much land, received only £210. A balance sheet presented at the 11th. June meeting shewed that for the first 21 miles of railway (to just beyond King's Langley) payment of £109,796 14s. 0d. had been authorized for a total of 345 acres 1 rood 6 perches of land; the sum authorized included compensation. The original estimate for the first 21 miles had been £98,296 14s. 0d. for 287 acres 3 roods 6 perches.

With all the necessary land in the possession of the Company, construction began. It was soon realized that the proposed Oxhey Lane Tunnel of eight chains length could be dispensed with, and a cutting substituted. In places the cutting is 40 feet deep, and the excavated material was taken northward to form part of the great embankment across the Colne Valley at Watford. The Oxhey Lane cutting is the largest earthwork on the line in the Harrow area. The Brent Viaduct* and embankment, on the southern boundary of the old Harrow Parish, is a close second.

The Schedule to the Nowells' contract gives some interesting details of 'Ballasting and Laying the Permanent Way' (The term 'permanent way', which is still used today, may have originated on the London & Birmingham. It was used to differentiate between the contractor's temporary tracks and the line as finished for permanent use.):

* The original Brent Viaduct, by the present Stonebridge Park Station, still survives and is listed Grade II.

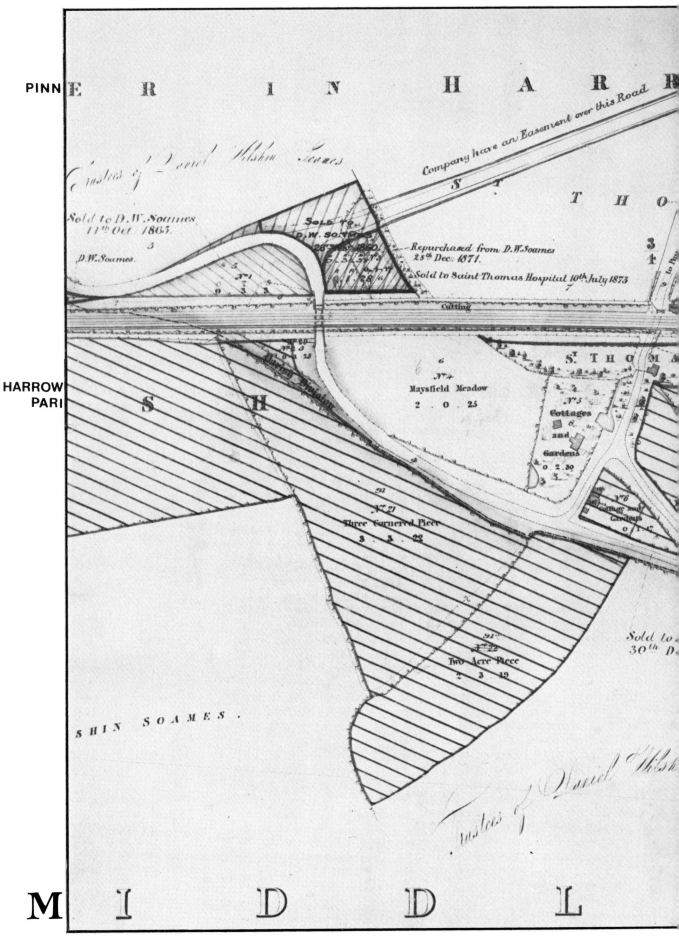

A section of the London & Birmingham Railway London Division *plan of 1840
(as revised by the LNWR in 1863) shewing the Pinner Park Crossing (centre of
plan) and Hatch End Farm area. The cross-hatched areas were subsequently sold
by the LNWR, but on Maysfield Meadow the 'Pinner Siding' was established; this
later became Hatch End Goods Yard. Headstone Lane Station, opened in 1913,*

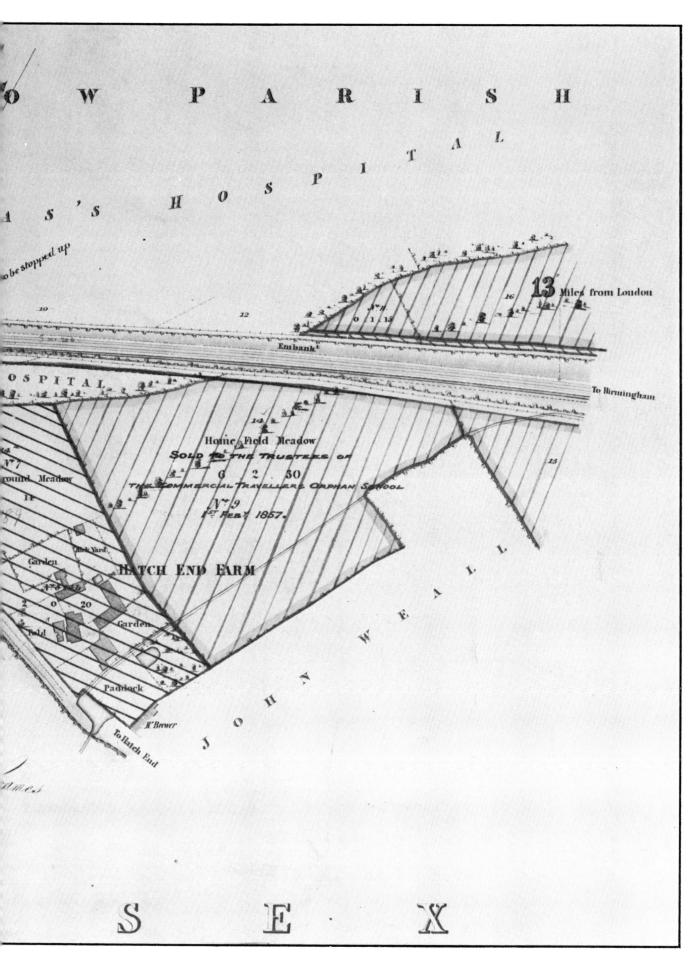

W PARISH

S'S HOSPITAL

to be stopped up

10

12

13 Miles from London

16

N°11

0 1 15

Embank.

OSPITAL

To Birmingham

14

Home Field Meadow

SOLD TO THE TRUSTEES OF

6   2   30

THE COMMERCIAL TRAVELLERS ORPHAN SCHOOL

N°9

1st Feb.y 1857.

N°7

round Meadow

15

1P

HATCH END FARM

Rick Yard

Garden

2   0   20

JOHN   WEALL

Garden

Field

Paddock

Mr Brewer

To Hatch End

ames

S E X

was built where the diverted course of Headstone Lane crosses the line on the left
side of the plan. The original survey was by Binns & Clifford, and is reproduced
here at the same slightly reduced scale as the Harrow Station plan on pages
38 and 39.

An example of permanent way laid on stone blocks, from George Findlay's The Working and Management of an English Railway. *The use of stone blocks was not a success, and the London & Birmingham sold them off to the Grand Junction Canal Company, who used them as coping stones on lock chambers.*
Peter G. Scott's collection.

The Railway is intended to form a double way composed of four single lines of Rails...

The Rails will be in lengths of from twelve to eighteen feet and weigh fifty pounds per lineal yard — they will be supported at every yard by a Cast Iron Chair or Pedestal which will weigh from fourteen to sixteen pounds and be accompanied by two wrought iron keys for fixing the rail in the Chair and two pins for fixing the Chair on the Sleeper or Block. The Sleepers will be of Wood and the Blocks of Stone or Wood...

The Company will reserve to themselves the right of directing whether Stone Blocks or Wood Sleepers shall be employed or both and if both in what proportion and situation.

The Material for Ballasting shall be composed of broken Stone or Clean Gravel entirely free from any admixture of Clay capable of setting hard and not retentive of moisture. If broken stone be used none shall be larger than Cubes of two inches square...

The Rails must be laid at the proper level or inclination each of them parallel and at the same height at any point...the two lines of way are to be six feet apart and the width between the insides of the Rails of each way four feet eight inches and a half.

The Rails Chairs Keys Pins Trenails Blocks and Sleepers shall be delivered to the Contractor at the nearest convenient canal Wharf which he may select but the Contractor shall be at the whole expense of removing them to any part of the line of Railway in the Contract.

It is likely that the Nowells had their materials delivered to Alperton Wharf on the Paddington Canal and Cassio Bridge Wharves on the Grand Junction Canal near Watford. Gravel for ballasting was taken locally, and the Nowells had a number of claims made against them for encroachment and illegally taking gravel.

The origin of the 4 feet 8½ inches gauge is interesting. Grooved roads or 'rutways' were known to classic Greece, and it is still possible to see the ruts that guided the Roman wagons in the streets of Pompeii. The Roman wagon wheels were 4 feet 8½ inches apart, and this was adopted as the Standard Gauge in Western Europe and North America. The Great Western Railway, however, had different ideas, and chose the even stranger gauge of 7 feet and a ¼ inch which was to hinder through traffic with other railways for many years. In 1834 the Great Western (whose line was then in the course of promotion) wanted to make a junction with the London & Birmingham at Kensal Green, with the intention that both railways would use the same London terminus. The London & Birmingham had already revived its plan for a station at Euston, and on 3rd. July, 1835, secured an Act authorizing the extension of its line from Camden Town to Euston Grove.* Two additional tracks into Euston were provided for the Great Western; but with that Company's subsequent adoption of the broad gauge, and the breakdown of negotiations over land for Great Western depots, the joint terminus never materialized. The Great Western went its own way to Paddington.

The construction of the railway was undoubtedly an upheaval for many inhabitants who lived close to the line. In *Dombey and Son* Charles Dickens gives a vivid impression of the London & Birmingham works at Camden Town:

"The first shock of a great earthquake had, just at that period, rent the whole neighbourhood to its centre. Traces of its course were visible on every side .... Here, a chaos of carts, overthrown and jumbled together, lay topsy-turvy at the bottom of a steep unnatural hill; there, confused treasures of iron soaked and rusted in something that had accidentally become a pond. Everywhere were bridges that led nowhere;

* The terminus was variously known as 'Euston Grove', 'Euston Square', or just plain 'Euston' in its early years. In timetables it often only appeared as 'London'.

thoroughfares that were wholly impassible; .... fragments of unfinished walls and arches, and piles of scaffolding, and wildernesses of bricks, and giant forms of cranes, and tripods straddling above nothing. There were a hundred thousand shapes and substances of imcompleteness ....

"In short, the yet unfinished and unopened Railroad was in progress; and, from the very core of all this dire disorder, trailed smoothly away, upon its mighty course of civilization and improvement."

And smoothly away it trailed to Harrow, where, on 24th. May, 1837, Pascoe St. L. Grenfell, a Director of the London & Birmingham Railway, made a report on the Harrow Contract for the London Committee:

"A single line is laid through the Watford Heath Cutting which is supplying ballast to other portions of the line. The Engine conveyed us from hence to No. 15 [Oxhey Lane]. We met Mr. Nowell at Watford Heath and I endeavoured to imprefs on him the necefsity of continued exertion in every way to get the work done. The Line may be laid in a very few days through No. 15 by which there will then be a line from Watford to No. 12 [Wembley]. The approaches at the Harrow Weall [sic] Bridge are still in a very backward state.

"At No. 12 the progrefs seemed more satisfactory. There were about 110 hands at work in the cutting and one line was to be through before they left off work that evening. The line of permanent way might be through in a week which will enable the engine to traverse the whole of the Contract on a single line which will be important from the want of ballast throughout it.

"From the Harrow Road on my way to London I could see that there remained a very small chasm to fill to close the Brent Embankment near the Bridge."

Lieutenant Peter Lecount, one of Robert Stephenson's 25 Assistant engineers, described the railway navvies as "banditti ... possessed of all the daring recklessness of the Smuggler, without any of his redeeming qualities,

Masons, navvies, bridge builders, and horses at work on the construction of the London & Birmingham Railway. These sketches were made by John C. Bourne.

Elton Collection, courtesy Ironbridge Gorge Museum.

A watercolour by C.J. Smith of Kenton Bridge at the time of the opening of the London & Birmingham Railway. It was here that Kenton Station was later to be built.

Heal Bequest, courtesy London Borough of Camden Local History Library.

their ferocious behaviour can only be equalled by the brutality of their language". The boys from Harrow School often met the navvies, and in the resulting affray the boys did not always come off worst as they were rather skillful at throwing stones. The Harrow Schoolboys even hitched illegal rides on the railway wagons, but a letter from Dr. Wordsworth, the Headmaster, to the London Committee soon put a stop to this practice.

On 29th. June, 1837, a party of Directors and friends made a successful trip from Euston to Box Moor* and back, and arrangements were made for experimental runs on 13th., 14th., 15th. and 17th. July. On each of these days 400 passengers would be conveyed, departing from Euston at 1.00 p.m. and 1.30 p.m. and returning in the same two trains from Box Moor at 4.00 p.m. and 4.30 p.m. The Directors and Sectretary could invite 20 persons each. Peers and Members of the House of Commons who had been friendly to the London & Birmingham Railway Company's Bills were also invited, along with other distinguished persons. On the first day a collation at Box Moor would be provided for 400 persons at 4/- per head.

The arrangements did not all run smoothly, for on 13th. July the first Up train suffered a delay after leaving the Watford Tunnel. This was "...occasioned by a Cock in the blast pipe of the engine being left open at Box Moor, and by the indifferent quality of some Coke supplied at that Station which it became necefsary to remove"; the early locomotives burned coke not coal. This same train also suffered an accident at Euston: its speed was

* The station here is now called 'Hemel Hempstead'.

22

not checked on entering the station, and the Brakesman was suspended from duty, but later reinstated by Robert Stephenson. The line from Camden Town into Euston is on a steep down gradient, as much as 1 in 70, due to the necessity to cross over the Regent's Canal at Camden Town. On trains leaving Euston, it was considered that the London & Birmingham's diminutive 2-2-0 locomotives (supplied under contract from Edward Bury) would not be able to cope with the gradient, so a stationary engine and ropes were installed to haul the trains up the incline. As this equipment was not ready at first, a powerful locomotive was hired from the Stephensons' locomotive works (Robert Stephenson & Co. of Newcastle upon Tyne) for banking trains up the incline until the stationary engine was ready.

On 17th. July 1837, the London Committee fixed the public opening to Box Moor for Thursday, 20th. July. The stations at Harrow and Watford would open for traffic at the same time. The timetable was as follows:

| Euston depart | 10 a.m., | 2 p.m., | 5 p.m., | 7 p.m. |
| Box Moor depart | 8 a.m., | 12 noon, | 4 p.m., | 6.30 p.m. |

Sundays:

| Euston depart | 7.30 a.m., | 9 a.m., | 5 p.m., | 7 p.m. |
| Box Moor depart | 7.30 a.m., | 5 p.m., | 7 p.m. | |

As early as 10th. January, 1834, the Reverend J. W. Cunningham, Vicar of Harrow, had urged the London & Birmingham's Directors "...to take every means in their power to prevent the introduction of Sunday travelling on the Railway". But with the advent of the new age of communication it was impossible to prevent Sunday travelling, although a 'Church Break' was a feature of many railway timetables until the beginning of this century. The London & Birmingham, however, did not forget the spiritual needs of its

An engraving entitled "Harrow on the Hill" from Thomas Roscoe's London & Birmingham Railway *(1839). This scene from the road bridge at Harrow Station was drawn by I. Wrightson and engraved by W. Radclyffe. Kenton Bridge is in the background.*
Harrow Local History Collection, London Borough of Harrow.

employees, and established a church and school at its Wolverton Works. Arrangements were also made by which each clerk and servant of the Company would have the opportunity of attending once on Sunday at church or chapel.

It seems that the summer of 1837 was a typically English one, and rather inclement for those passengers travelling in the open 3rd. class trucks. At the London Committee meeting on 6th. September it was stated that "...the Slips in Embankment No. 15 [near Oxhey Lane] of the Harrow Contract have given way so much since the late rains as to endanger the stability of the Road, that it is of great importance that Me*f*srs. Nowell should immediately take steps to secure them as well as to complete the slopes of Embankment No. 16 [in the Colne Valley] ...." The Committee agreed that the Nowells should complete their contract immediately.

The first two pages of Lloyd's London and Birmingham Railway Guide *(1838) describing the journey from Euston to Watford.*

Peter G. Scott's collection.

LONDON & BIRMINGHAM
Railway Guide.

–•••••—

With full particulars of every object on the line of Road on both sides, and description of all the

TOWNS, STATIONS, FARES,

AND

TIMES OF STARTING, &c. &c.

ALSO FULL DIRECTIONS FOR PROCEEDING TO

MANCHESTER & LIVERPOOL

BY THE

RAILWAY.

–•••••—

LONDON STATION, EUSTON SQUARE.

The London Terminus of this important Railway is at Euston Grove, near Euston Square, in the New Road. This grand, but simple structure is from the design of Philip Hardwick, Esq., the architect of St. Katherine's Docks, Goldsmiths Hall, the City Club House, &c. The facade occupies about 300 feet towards Drummond Street, opposite a wide opening in Euston Square.

The principal elevation, as shown in the engraving, consists of a Grecian Doric portico in antœ, with two lodges on each side, appropriated to the offices of the company; the spaces between the columns and antœ of the portico, and also of the lodges, being inclosed by very handsome, massive iron gates. The whole is executed in masonry and of stone from the Bramley Fall Quarries, in Yorkshire.

Leaving the Station yard at Euston Grove, and passing Chalk Farm Lane, the trains arrive at

BUILDING THE LINE THROUGH HARROW

On 16th. October, 1837, the line was extended to Tring; and on 9th. April, 1838, to Denbigh Hall, where the railway crossed Watling Street just beyond Bletchley. Also on 9th. April the section of line between Rugby and Birmingham was opened. So that a through service could be provided as soon as possible, the London & Birmingham contracted the famous coaching firm of Chaplin & Horne to operate a road coach service between Denbigh Hall and Rugby in connexion with the railway. On 17th. September, 1838, the line was opened throughout, and the road coaches were withdrawn. There was thus inaugurated the first train service to connect London with another great centre of population. It was a day of celebration, and all the men in the Company's employ were allowed a gratuity not exceeding one day's pay (the average weekly wage was about 20/- to 25/-).

A profusion of 'Railway Guides' and 'Companions' were published;

---

2   THE RAILWAY GUIDE.

PRIMROSE HILL TUNNEL,

one mile and a half from London. This is a most stupendous work, 1120 yards in length, and which occupied three years in its formation. Much has been said of the nuisance arising from passing through tunnels but experience has proved that with the exception of the temporary darkness, and a slight change in the atmosphere there is nothing to which the most fastidious or delicate traveller can object. At

KILBURN,

the line passes under the Edgware Road, on emerging from which the road proceeds to

KENSAL GREEN,

where is another Tunnel 320 yards in length. On the left of it is the General Cemetery, where, upon a beautiful enclosure tastefully disposed and secure from depredation, a public company have established the first mortuary of its kind in the vicinity of the metropolis. At six miles from London is Lower Place, and one mile further on is

THE BRENT RIVER VIADUCT,

from which place to the first station at Harrow we proceed through the diversified and richly cultivated country for which the immediate neighbourhood of the metropolis is so eminent.

On the left of the road is the town of Harrow so celebrated for its school at which many of our most distinguished statesmen were educated.

HARROW WEALD, *(Station.)*

the first halting place on this line, is distant about eleven miles and a quarter from London. Proceeding onwards we pass Hatch End, and just before reaching the fourteenth mile, enter the county of Hertford, at Bushey Heath. The great Watford Tunnel, with its lofty shafts, next appears in view. This tunnel is nearly a mile in length, and is one of the most extraordinary efforts of engineering skill that can be imagined. The average time occupied in passing through is two minutes and a half.

WATFORD,

sixteen miles from London, is situated on the River Colne, about three miles distant from Rickmansworth, and was so called from *Wet* and *Ford* at the south end of the town, where was a ford over the river. The prætorian, or consular way, made by the Romans, and called Watling Street, crosses the Colne near it, and passes on to Verulam, near St. Albans. The town consists of one very long street, which is extremely dirty in the winter, and the waters of the river at the entrance of the town are often so much swelled by the floods as to be impassable.

Close to the town is Cashisbury Park, the seat of the Earl of Essex,

extracts from Lloyd's *London and Birmingham Railway Guide* are reproduced on pages 24-26. In Osborne's Guide, published under the same title, the writer got a little carried away, describing the London & Birmingham as:

"... a piece of human workmanship of the most stupendous kind; which, when considered with respect to its scientific character, magnitude, utility, its harmony of arrangement, and mechanical contrivance, eclipses all former works of art. Compared to it, how shabby a structure would be the celebrated Roman wall, or even the more extensive one of the Chinese; as for the Egyptian pyramids, they, so far from being fit to be mentioned in comparison with the railway, are merely uncouth monuments of the ignorance and superstition of their founders...."

The timetable from Lloyd's London and Birmingham Railway Guide *for 1838 before the line was completed between Denbeigh* (sic) *Hall and Rugby.*

Peter G. Scott's collection.

8

THE RAILWAY GUIDE.

THE FOLLOWING, UNTIL FURTHER NOTICE, WILL BE THE TIMES FOR THE DEPARTURE OF THE TRAINS (EXCEPT ON SUNDAY):—

	From London.	From Denbeigh Hall by Coach to Rugby.	From Rugby.	
DOWN.	7½ a. m.	10 a. m.	2½ p. m.	to Birmingham.
	9¼ a. m.	12 a. m.	4½ p. m.	to do.
	†11 a. m.			to Denbeigh Hall.
	1 p. m.	3½ p. m.	8 p. m	to Birmingham.
	†3 p. m.			to Denbeigh Hall.
	†5 p. m.			to do.
	8½ p. m.			to do. (Mail.)
	From Birmingham.	**From Rugby by Coach to Denbeigh Hall**	**From Denbeigh Hall.**	
UP.	——	——	4 a. m.	to London (Mail)
	——	——	†7 a. m.	to do.
	——	——	†9½ a. m.	to do.
	9 a. m.	10½ a. m.	3 p. m.	to do.
	——	——	†5 p. m.	to do.
	12 a. m.	1½ p. m.	6 p. m.	to do.
	1½ a. m.	3 p. m.	7½ p. m.	to do.

ON SUNDAYS.

	From London.	From Denbeigh Hall by Coach to Rugby.	From Rugby.	
DOWN.	7½ a.m.	10 a.m.	2½ p.m.	to Birmingham.
	†9½ a.m.	——	——	to Denbeigh Hall.
	†5 p.m.	——	——	to do.
	8½ p.m.	——	——	to do. (Mail.)
	From Birmingham.	**From Rugby by Coach to Denbeigh Hall.**	**From Denbeigh Hall.**	
UP.	——	——	4 a.m.	to London (Mail.)
	——	——	†7½ a.m.	to do.
	——	——	†5 p.m.	to do.
	1½ p.m.	3 p.m.	7½ p.m.	to do.

The trains marked thus † are those which stop for passengers at Harrow Boxmoor, and Berkhampstead Stations; the remaining trains between Denbeigh Hall and London, stopping at Watford, Tring and Leighton.

N. B: An additional train between Rugby and Birmingham is now put on. It leaves Rugby, (Sundays excepted)at nine a. m. and returns from Birmingham at six p. m. stopping at Coventry to take up and set down passengers.

BUILDING THE LINE THROUGH HARROW

The total cost of constructing the 112½ mile line was £5,698,375; or £50,652 per mile. The revised estimate of the cost of the Harrow Contract was £144,574.

There has been some confusion in the past over the date that the first passenger train ran throughout from Euston to Birmingham. The date given above, 17th. September, 1838, *is* correct. There are earlier references in the London & Birmingham's Committee of Management and London Committee minutes which mention 'through trains', but on careful reading of these minutes it becomes obvious that the Company referred to the train/road coach/train connexions as 'through trains', and hence the confusion.

Harrow was the first station from Euston, and Watford the second, but they were soon to be joined by others at Wilsdon (where the railway somehow adopted the *16th.* century spelling 'Willesden'), Sudbury, Pinner, and Bushey. The stations at Sudbury and Pinner were in the Harrow and Pinner parishes respectively, so we will briefly examine their origins before looking at Harrow Station in more detail in the next chapter.

Most of the early stations were named after the nearest large village or town, and not after the place where they were actually situated. We should therefore note here that Sudbury Station was in Wembley (then often spelt without the second 'e') and Pinner Station was by the Dove House Farm at Woodridings.

Harrow School had belatedly objected to the siting of Harrow Station and instead wanted a station at Wembley where the Harrow Road crossed the line. Harrow Station had already been constructed, but the London & Birmingham agreed to keep in mind a station at the Harrow Road should the need arise.

On 20th. April, 1842, the Coaching & Police Committee received a "Memorial from 79 Inhabitants of Pinner, Ruislip, &c., praying for the establishment of a Station either at the Dove House Bridge or the Pinner Park Cro*f*sing". We have already mentioned the Pinner Park Crossing earlier in this chapter; the Dove House Bridge was just to the north, and carried the Great Stanmore — Pinner Green road (the Uxbridge Road) over the line. On 13th. May, 1842, the London & Birmingham's Board of Directors resolved that stations should be established at the Harrow Road Bridge and at Pinner Park Crossing. However, shortly afterwards, on 25th. May, the Coaching & Police committee resolved that the station at Pinner Park Crossing should instead be established at the Dove House Bridge.

Once the decision had been taken to erect the new stations no time was wasted. On 1st. June, 1842, the Coaching & Police Committee approved the estimates of the costs: £60 for the station at the Dove House Bridge and £180 for the station at the Harrow Road Bridge. They were obviously to be very modest structures, particularly that at the Dove House Bridge. At its 9th. June meeting the Committee objected to the Harrow Road Bridge Station being called by that name, "...there being already a Harrow Station, and to propose either 'Wembley' or 'Sudbury' as the name". Inevitably they were to choose the wrong one — Sudbury. The name chosen for the Dove House Bridge Station was 'Pinner', 1½ miles away.

A report of the Coaching & Police Committee dated 10th. June, 1842, gives the *single* fares to and from the new stations:

	1st. Class	2nd. Class	3rd. Class
London to & from Pinner	3s. 6d.	2s. 6d.	1s. 6d.
———— " ———— Harrow Road Bridge	2s. 6d.	1s. 6d.	1s. -

A Coaching & Police Committee minute of 3rd. August, 1842, records that Sudbury Station was to open on 8th. August, 1842; but no mention is made of Pinner Station. A later minute dated 15th. February 1843, mentions arrangements for booking passengers from Pinner to the next Down station, but from reading this minute it is obvious that Pinner Station was already open. It can only be assumed, therefore, that Pinner Station also opened on 8th. August, 1842, and the scribe writing the minutes unintentionally omitted Pinner Station from the 3rd. August minute. A search through the columns of the 'local' newspaper of the time, the *County Herald & Weekly Advertiser* (which circulated "250 Miles Round London"), did not reveal any more information, and for some reason both Pinner and Sudbury did not appear in *Bradshaw's Railway Guide* until the 1844 edition.*

Over the years, Pinner and Sudbury stations have seen many changes, particularly in their names. Sudbury became Sudbury & Wembley on 1st. May, 1882, then Wembley for Sudbury on 1st. November, 1910, and finally Wembley Central on 5th. July, 1948. The station itself is now a somewhat depressing claustrophobic place with a shopping precinct, flats, and offices spanning the tracks.

Pinner Station was renamed Pinner & Hatch End on 1st. January, 1897, then Hatch End for Pinner on 1st. February, 1920, and finally Hatch End on 11th. June, 1956. It is worth noting, however, that the nearest station to Hatch End proper is the present *Headstone Lane* Station — indeed, on LNWR Parliamentary Plans the bridge carrying Headstone Lane over the line is marked as '*Hatch End* Bridge'. The present Hatch End Station should really be called Woodridings.

In 1911 Pinner & Hatch End Station was rebuilt to the design of Gerald Horsley, and is described as a "little gem" by Gordon Biddle and O. S. Nock in *The Railway Heritage of Britian*. The entrance block, with Romanesque arches and a cupola, is listed Grade II by the Department of the Environment as being of Special Architectural or Historic Interest.

* Printed works usually give the date '1844' or '*circa* 1844' for the opening of Pinner Station (and sometimes for Sudbury as well). This is obviously based on *Bradshaw* but is incorrect.

Two pages from the London & Birmingham Railway's Working Time Table for May, 1841. Each train is listed individually, and a note inserted where another passenger train is running on the same line just ahead of the one listed. Note the ten minute stop at Wolverton for passengers to take refreshment.

Public Record Office, RAIL 981/243.

84			85		
1½ P.M.					
UP Train.			5¾ hours — London time.		
SUNDAYS.					
FROM BIRMINGHAM			TO LONDON.		
STATIONS.	TIME.		STATIONS.	TIME.	
	HOURS.	MINUTES.		HOURS.	MINUTES.
Leaves . **Birmingham**	1	40	Leaves . **Wolverton** .	4	45
Arrives at **Hampton** ..	2	0	Arrives at **Bletchley** .	5	0
„ **Coventry** ..	2	25	„ **Leighton** ..	5	16
„ **Brandon** ..	2	42	„ ***Tring**	5	45
„ **Rugby**	3	0	„ **Bᵏ.hampstᵈ**.	5	57
„ **Crick**	3	26	„ **Boxmoor** ..	6	7
„ **Weedon** ...	3	40	„ **Kgˢ Langley**	6	15
„ **Blisworth** .	4	3	„ **Watford** ..	6	24
„ **Roade**	4	13	„ **Harrow** ...	6	42
„ **Wolverton** .	4	35	„ **Camden** ...	7	8
			„ **Euston**	7	15

* **Note.**—A Train leaves Aylesbury at **5** o'clock to meet this Train from Birmingham, reaching Tring at **5 . 30**.

2 HARROW STATION, 1837–1987

"The Harrow Station has a cistern to supply the engine with water, if required, and an office and waiting-room, with clerk, porters, &c. A road branches off to Stanmore, Edgeware, &c., to the north, and to Harrow, Pinner, &c., to the south and west. The village [sic] of Harrow on the Hill is remarkable for its great public school, and for the conical form and insular features of the eminence which give it name."

    John Britton writing in John C. Bourne's
    Drawings of the London & Birmingham Railway
    (Bourne, Ackerman, & Tilt, 1839).

Harrow Station has undergone many changes in its 150 year history. It was originally a small wayside station situated on the road between the hamlets of Greenhill (¾ mile distant) and Harrow Weald (1 mile distant). There was nothing much else in the vicinity of the station except for the Queen's Arms public house. The station was originally named 'Harrow Weald', and was designated by the London & Birmingham Railway as an 'Intermediate Station' which meant that only 2nd. class, 3rd. class or mixed-class trains stopped there. The first 'Principal Station' from London, which served also 1st. class and mail trains, was at Watford. (It is interesting to note that the original Watford Station still survives next to the Saint Albans Road bridge; it is the only extant London & Birmingham intermediate station and is listed Grade II.)

At Harrow Weald the plans for the modest single-storey station building were approved by the London Committee on 8th. March, 1837. Thomas Jackson of Number 1 Wharf, Commercial Road, Pimlico, signed an Indenture dated 22nd. March, 1837, with the London & Birmingham Railway, agreeing to build the Harrow Weald Station for the sum of £663. Only two months were allowed for the station's completion; it had to be ready by 22nd. May. The Indenture records that if any question or dispute should arise between Thomas Jackson and the railway company, "...the same shall be referred to the Award and determination of Philip Hardwick of Ruſsell Square in the County of Middlesex, Achitect, whose decision shall be final and without appeal". Philip Hardwick is probably best remembered for his great 'Doric Arch' at Euston, the fate of which is mentioned in Chapter 9.

The Schedule to Thomas Jackson's contract contains a "Specification of the Works to be done and the Materials used in erecting the Office Walls and Piers and Enclosure under the Water Tank at the Harrow Weald Station of the London & Birmingham Railway". It demands that the best materials of their several kinds should be used. The English Oak had to be sound, well seasoned, and free of sap or shakes, and similarly the fir and deals from the Baltic had to be well seasoned, free of sap, shakes, or large or dead knots. Best quality stock bricks were to be used, and the facing of all the work in sight had to be "picked of an uniform color with square edges". The lime had to be from Dorking or Merstham, or any stone lime of equal quality. (The lime works at Merstham was served by the Croydon, Merstham & Godstone Iron Railway, an extension of the pioneer Surrey Iron Railway; see 'Mileposts' on page 8.)

The Specification runs to 12 pages, and includes general details of the station's foundations and bricklaying, including instructions to the Digger for constructing a "ceſspool in half brick laid dry under the privies". Instructions are also given to the Carpenter and Joiner, the Mason, the Plumber, the Slater, the Plasterer, the Painter, the Glazier, and the Smith and Founder (for rain water pipes and iron railings). One of the painter's tasks was to prime the stucco Inscription Tablets with red lead and oil, paint them with four coats of 'stone color', and then write "London & Birmingham Railway" on the tablets in a "shadowed 6 inch letter of color and form to be approved". Also included in the Specification are details for the construction of a coke house under the water tank.

A plan of the original layout of Harrow Weald Station has been prepared, and is reproduced on page 31. It is based on John C. Bourne's drawing and

1 Wharf, Commercial Road
Pimlico
Mar: 15. 1837.

To the London Committee of Directors of the London and Birmingham Railway Company.

Gentlemen,

I will engage to build the Harrow Weald Station agreeably to the Drawings and Specification for the sum of Six hundred and sixty three pounds.

I have the honor to be, Gentlemen,

Your very Obed.t Serv.t

Tho.s Jackson.

£663.

19

Thomas Jackson's agreement to build Harrow Weald Station, appended to the Contract.
Public Record Office, RAIL 584/177.

a contemporary sketch by C. J. Smith (both reproduced on page 33), the plans of the *London & Birmingham Railway London Division* (1840), and the map that accompanies J. Tootell's *Valuation of the Parish of Harrow* (1852). The 1840 survey was carried out by Binns & Clifford of Birmingham, but was revised by the LNWR in 1863. The section relating to Harrow Station is reproduced on pages 38 and 39. By a careful study of the erasures and revisions on the original plan, and comparing them with the 1852 valuation map, it has been possible to create a fairly accurate picture of the original station. It will be noted that the station building and entrance are on the Harrow Weald (east) side of the line, in agreement with the station's original name. It has been often thought, and previously written, that the original station building was on the west side, but this was not so.

As briefly mentioned in the previous chapter, Harrow School did not express an opinion on the coming of the railway until the Harrow Weald Station had already been built. In June and July, 1837, letters were sent to the London Committee from Dr. Wordsworth (Headmaster of Harrow School), Henry Young (Secretary to the School Governors), the Reverend J. W. Cunningham, and Masters of Harrow School, expressing the opinion that the station should be fixed at Wembley as a station at Harrow Weald "...may be injurious to the discipline of the School". The London & Birmingham replied that a station at Wembley would be inconvenient for its passengers from Harrow, and would be no less injurious to the School's discipline. It is impossible to believe that Harrow School hoped to achieve anything by objecting to the position of the station only a few days before the line was due to open. (The only other possible site for a station had been on the Tyburn Lane towards Kenton — where Kenton Station was later built, — but this

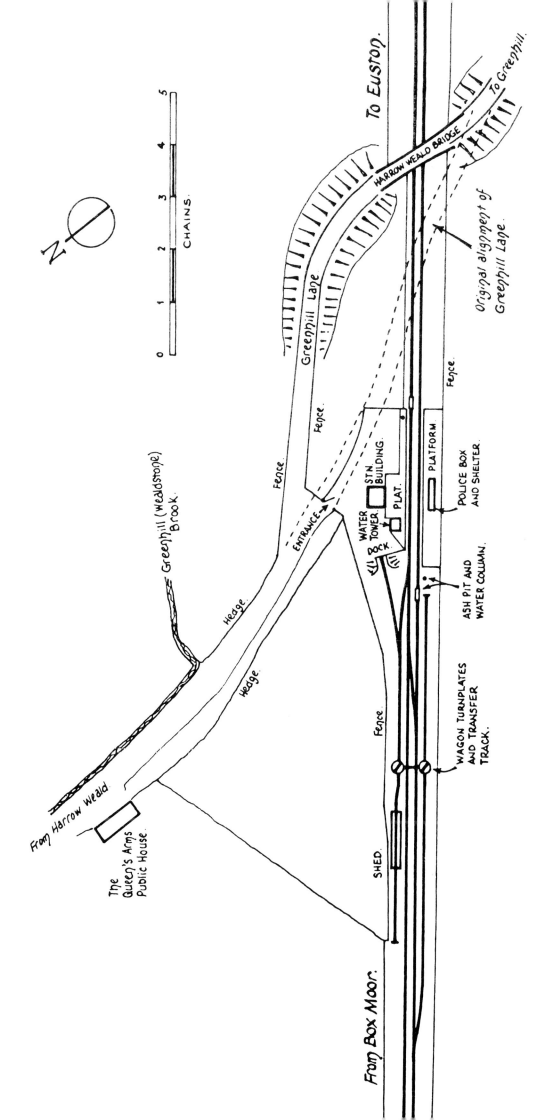

Harrow Weald Station ~ London & Birmingham Railway ~ 1837.

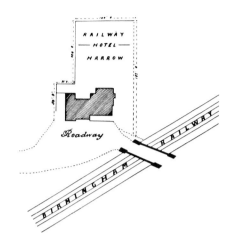

Railway Hotel conveyance plan, dated 11th. July, 1884.

Courtesy Watney Combe Reid & Co. Ltd.

lane was nothing more than a muddy farm track between fields and quite unsuitable for access.)

On 20th. July, 1837, Harrow Weald Station opened for passenger and goods traffic, with trains running between Euston and Box Moor. So many people travelled to the new station (it was the first stop from Euston) that the Queen's Arms, being the only place of refreshment nearby, was so overwhelmed with customers that beer was drawn in buckets and ladled out to the thirsty passengers.

The Reverend W. W. Phelps, a Master at Harrow School, recorded in his diary* for 31st. July, 1837, "First saw train on the railroad at the Weald", and on 2nd. August, "It is a great diversion to go down to the railroad station and see the arrival of a train. We saw about four hundred persons brought up at the rate of thirty miles an hour by one train and engine". On 4th. August the Reverend Phelps went to London on the train for the first time. The journey took about 30 minutes.

The original fares between London, Harrow, and Watford are quoted in the London Committee's minutes as follows:

	1st.	2nd.	3rd.
London to Harrow 11½ miles	2/6	2/-	1/-
Harrow to Watford 6 miles	1/6	1/-	1/-

It was at the time of opening, or soon afterwards, that the name of Harrow Weald Station was shortened to 'Harrow' (that town being 1½ miles distant to the south beyond Greenhill). In 1838, however, there are still some references to 'Harrow Weald Station' in Railway Guides and the London & Birmingham minutes. A curious feature of the early days was that stations kept Local Time and not 'London Time'. The clock at Harrow Station was one minute slower than that at Euston; at Birmingham the clock was 7¼ minutes slower.

In January, 1838, it was proposed to lease a portion of the railway land at Harrow Station for the erection of a tavern. It does not, however, appear on any maps, and was probably never built. The present Railway Hotel (also previously known as the Railway Station Hotel or Railway Tavern) which is situated next to the road bridge on the west side of the line, was built on land bought in 1853 from a local farmer, Henry Finch Hill.

In May, 1938, the Reverend J. W. Cunningham again appears in the London & Birmingham's minutes. This time he had written to the Committee of Management wishing to know whether it could be so arranged that the through (1st. class) trains stop at Harrow upon a given signal, "...and if not would the first Friday train be allowed to stop a few Minutes for some Pa∫sengers from Birmingham". The Committee replied that they could not deviate from the general rule, but would bear the application in mind in their future arrangements. It was not until further complaints about the poor service had been made that Harrow Station was raised to 'first-class status' in 1850. This meant that 1st. class and mail trains also called, but the service was still sparse. There was, for example, a mid-morning interval in the Down direction of over 3½ hours without a train.

Complaints about fares are also nothing new. In 1838 the 1st. class fare from Euston to Harrow was increased by 6d. to 3/-. (It was possible to travel 1st. class to Harrow in a mixed-class train.) On 23rd. March, 1838, a Mr. Pearson transmitted "a memorial from Inhabitants of Harrow and vicinity for a reduction of the fares". The Committee of Management, however, did not think it expedient to make any alterations.

In August, 1838, the future philosopher, Herbert Spencer, had an interesting escapade on a train through Harrow. At this time he was only eighteen years of age and was employed as an engineer on the London & Birmingham Railway. He worked under Charles Fox, who was Resident Engineer for the London Division of the line, extending from Euston to

* As related by Charles Hole in *Life of The Rev. & Ven. William Whitmarsh Phelps, M.A.* Vol. II (1873).

John C. Bourne's drawing of the Harrow Weald Bridge in May, 1837. Only one line of track has been laid, and the Greenhill Lane crosses it on the level in the foreground. The road approaches to the bridge have yet to be constructed. The view is looking towards Euston, and the Harrow Weald station building is situated behind the artist. This photograph is of the original drawing which was hanging in the London Midland Region Assistant General Manager's office at Stanier House, Birmingham. Along with other Bourne originals, it is due to be removed to the National Railway Museum at York.

 Photograph by Mel Figures, courtesy British Rail, London Midland Region.

A sketch by C.J. Smith of the Harrow Weald Station slightly later in 1837, again looking towards Euston. The station building is on the left, and next to it is the water tower on which a workman appears to be putting the finishing touches. The train is standing on the 'wrong' line, but may be a works train unloading materials. It appears that space for the ground-level Down-side platform has not yet been cleared, and there is also no water crane. The two horses in the Reverend J.W. Cunningham's field are viewing the new 'iron horse' with some scepticism.

 Heal Bequest, courtesy London Borough of Camden Local History Library.

An unbraked coach-truck.
Courtesy Railway Gazette.

Wolverton. One day in early August Herbert Spencer was sent to Wolverton Station (due to open the following month) to make a survey. The station was just a short distance beyond the temporary terminus at Denbigh Hall, and it is evident that trains were running to Wolverton in order to turn around. The Company's main works were also established there, and this may have been the reason for the survey.

Spencer finished his work in time to catch the last London-bound train, timetabled to leave Denbigh Hall at 7.30 p.m. He was living at Wembley, so his nearest station was Harrow, but the 7.30 train ran non-stop from Watford to London. He saw a way round this problem by asking the Station Master at Wolverton to attach a spare truck to the rear of the train. His plan was to ride in this truck from Watford, and on the approach to Harrow he would slip the coupling and bring the truck to a stand in Harrow Station. There was only one problem; the only spare vehicle available at Wolverton was a coach-truck with *no brakes*. (Coach-trucks were used to convey gentlemen's private road-coaches on the railway.)

All went to plan as far as the Dove House Bridge, two miles north of Harrow Station, where he uncoupled the truck from the rest of the train. Spencer knew that the line through Harrow was on a 1 in 339 downward gradient, and he considered that two miles should be a sufficient distance for the truck to stop. He was wrong. He sailed through Harrow Station at 30 miles an hour less than a dozen yards behind the train! The truck managed to lose some of its velocity on the curve by Woodcock Hill, but still the truck rolled onwards. He passed an astonished platelayer who thought it was a new invention, and then in an effort to stop the truck he wedged a crossbar against one of the wheels. This involved leaning over the side of the vehicle so much that he had to give it up for fear of falling out.

By now he was crossing the River Brent, nearly 4½ miles from Harrow. Spencer was frightened that he would crash through the Willesden Level Crossing gates and be killed, but the downwards gradient came to an end and the truck stopped in the middle of the embankment crossing the Brent Valley. He walked forward to Willesden and managed to persuade the level crossing keeper (who did not believe his story) to help him push the truck back to the Brent Siding, which was situated just north of the Brent Viaduct. After derailing the truck on the points, they eventually managed to get it clear of the main line in readiness for the next day's traffic. Everybody who witnessed this escapade had a good laugh at Herbert Spencer's expense. He later gave up his engineering career, and went on to become a journalist and then a great philosopher. It was he who coined the phrase "the survival of the fittest", obviously not forgetting his reckless attempt at stopping a truck in Harrow Station.

In 1841 Thomas Jackson, the builder of Harrow Station, won a further contract for the erection of a house and four cottages next to the station building. The cost was £881. Robert Stephenson had, in fact, approved plans for the cottages four years earlier. The London & Birmingham and the North Western built many cottages for their railway workers so there would always be platelayers and others close at hand for fog signalling duties. By 1852 a larger house for the Station Master had been built, and this survived the 1858 rebuilding of the station whereas the earlier dwellings did not.

In 1844 an addition to the platform at Harrow Station was approved, and in February, 1845, new coal sidings and a goods depot were ordered. A goods shed was erected immediately to the north of the station building where there had previously been an end-loading dock. This supplemented an existing narrow coal transfer shed provided when the line opened.

The discipline of the Harrow School boys at the station is mentioned in the North Western's Coaching & Police Committee (Traffic) minutes of 17th. February, 1847. Dr. Vaughan, the Headmaster, had written to the Company stating that he had "...taken means for preventing a repetition of the recent irregularity in some of the Harrow Scholars who pelted the Trains with Snow Balls". He suggested that in future no boys should be booked at the station

unless they produced an authority from a Master.

Towards the end of 1853 the LNWR made an attempt at attracting building development near its stations within easy reach of London. The following item appeared in *The Builder* giving brief details:

"The London and North-Western Company have announced that they will give a free first-class pass for a series of years to persons who will build houses worth not less than 50*l*. per ann. at Harrow, Pinner, Bushey, Watford, King's Langley, Boxmoor, Berkhampstead, or Tring."

A register was kept of all the house passes issued: the first pass went to Edward Penrose Hathaway of Harrow for 11 years from 1st. July, 1854. The passes were issued for a particular house, so if that property changed hands the pass was re-issued in the new owner's name.

In 1858 an article entitled "Harrow New Town" appeared in *The Builder*, and this was reprinted in the *Harrow Gazette & General Advertiser*, 1st. June edition:

"Amongst the numerous country stations which are being converted into ornamental villages by the increasing longings of metropolitan men for a home in the fresh air and green fields, it is only to be expected that the long-esteemed locality of Harrow on the Hill, eleven miles and a half from London, should take a prominent place. The privileges accorded to residents in respect of Harrow School are of themselves sufficient to give the locality a preference with that numerous class of London men, in easy circumstances, whose most cherished possessions, after all, are their children; and apart from all considerations of the salubrity of the place, would be sufficient to account for what we are told as the fact, that the applications for residences from 50*l*. to 120*l*. a year of rental are so numerous as to make it no insignificant part of the duty of the obliging station-master of the railway to explain that there are none to be had. The old town of Harrow being a mile and a half from the railway station, the new town is springing up around the station itself. Large estates of building land have been brought into application, and considerable sums of money laid out in roads and drainage. Several villas have already been built, and a number of smaller houses. Water has been laid on by the public company of the neighbourhood, and gas is offered by the Harrow Gas

This view was drawn by an unknown artist in 1853 to accompany a sale brochure for the Headstone Farm estate, and shews the new railway bridge over Pinner Drive (later renamed Headstone Drive). The 2-2-2 locomotive and train have just left Harrow Station, but appear to be running on the wrong line. Note that all the trucks have six wheels instead of four.
Harrow Local History Collection, London Borough of Harrow.

L. & N. W. R.—HOUSE PASSES.

No. on Register   **47.**

Situation of House   Roxeth nr Harrow

Name of Owner   Revd Cunningham

Pass granted for   **11**   Years from   1st July 1859.

Name of Occupier.	No. of Pass.	Date. From	Date. To	REMARKS.
R Sweeting	5544	1 July 1859	31 Decr 1859	
	6321	1 Jany 1860	31 Decr 1860	
	8932	1 Jany. 1861	31 Decr 1861	
	1607	1 Jany 1862	31 Decr 1862	retd & cancelled 30/9/62.
J. Morgan Knott		1 Octr 1862	31 Decr 1862	
	5227	1 Jany 1863	31 Decr 1863.	
	30	1 Jany 1864	31 Dec 1864	
	33	1 Jany 1865	31 Dec 1865	
	29	1 Jany 1866	31 Dec 1866	retd & canc 19/8/66.
Revd Wm Horne. ————		1 Septr 1866	31 Decr 1866	
	260	1 Jany 1867	31 Dec 1867.	add "Sudbury"
	820	1 Jany 1868	31 Decr 1868.	
	1476	1 Jany 1869	31 Dec 1869.	
	2,185	1 Jany 1870	30 June 1870	Includes Sudbury.

The Reverend J.W. Cunningham obtained an LNWR House Pass for 'The Parsonage' on London Hill, Roxeth (next to Christ Church). This is a copy of the entry in the Free House Passes register.

Public Record Office, RAIL 410/1242.

Works, as well as by the Railway Company. Sewerage also has been begun. In the largest of the building estates, the Headstone Farm, of 500 acres, under the control of Mr. Edwin Fox, a bridge has been built under the railway; and two fine avenues planted on each side with trees, have been formed, of the length of a mile in one instance (Harrow View), and three-quarters of mile in another (Pinner Drive*). The old farm road† of the estate, over a mile in length, is also to be widened, to correspond with the others, and various other lines of roads are laid out. These roads have been so formed, as to levels, that the drainage is a simple matter, which is not always the case. These and the bridge are by Mr. Kerr, of London, architect. Several smaller estates have been laid out.

"The London and North-Western Railway Company offers, as an encouragement to building, a free first-class ticket, for eleven years, to every occupier of a new house above 50*l.* a year in value, — a wise liberality."

The train service remained inadequate, however, and was hardly an incentive to would-be season ticket holders travelling daily to London. By 1864, Canning, Peel, Palmerston, Byron, Oxford, and Marlborough roads were also well established (although the latter two were not named), but there were only a handful of houses in all these roads together. The name 'Harrow New Town' was thankfully not perpetuated, and the small settlement around Harrow Station was called 'Station End'. (The Calvinistic Baptists' Station End Chapel in Palmerston Road survives today as the Salvation Army Citadel.)

Eventually the name 'Wealdstone' was adopted by the community. There was a Wealdstone House and a Wealdstone Farm at Harrow Weald, and the 'Weald Stone', thought to be an ancient boundary stone, is situated outside the Red Lion public house.

The issue of house passes was discontinued after 1st. August, 1867, except where application had been made before that date for houses which would be occupied by 1st. August, 1869. From Harrow to Tring the total number of properties for which house passes were issued was 208. It was hardly a success story.

One of the reasons why the local train service was so poor was the congestion caused by long distance traffic on the two-track main line. In order to bring some relief, an Up Goods line was brought into use in 1858 between Watford and the west end of the Primrose Hill Tunnel. This line threaded its way around the east side of Harrow Station, but involved the demolition of the goods shed and the original station building, cottages, and house. A new station building in yellow brick Italianate style was erected slightly nearer to the road. The Up Goods line effectively cut off the station building from the Up and Down platforms, so a footbridge was provided in the middle of the station. The original station never had a footbridge; to reach the Down platform passengers had had to cross the tracks on the level.

A new goods shed was erected in the yard (the shed survived, with a later extension, until 1969), and five new railwaymen's cottages were built next to the Queen's Arms. Land at the rear of the Queen's Arms had been bought from Thomas Clutterbuck (owner of Clutterbuck's Brewery on Stanmore Hill) for an extension to the coal yard, and a vegetable oil gas plant had commenced operations here in 1852. All these alterations and additions are shewn on the 1840 London & Birmingham Railway plan, as amended in 1863. Also shewn is the new railway bridge constructed to allow Headstone Drive to pass under the tracks.

In March, 1868, Mr. W. Tew, the local Delivery Agent to the LNWR, wrote to the *Harrow Gazette* suggesting that street nameplates should be erected as it was difficult for strangers to find the whereabouts of residents. Enamelled

* Pinner Drive was shortly afterwards called Headstone Drive.
† Named Pinner View.

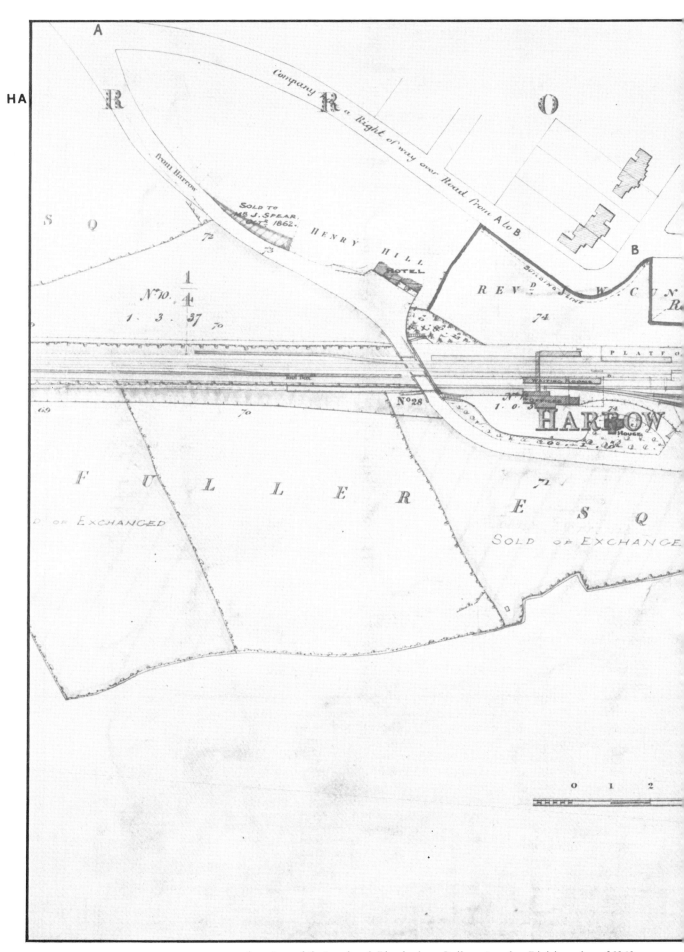

A section of the London & Birmingham Railway London Division *plan of 1840 (as revised by the LNWR in 1863) shewing Harrow Station with the Up Goods line on the east side. The original plan was by Binns & Clifford, and is reproduced here at a slightly reduced scale.*

Public Record Office, RAIL 384/191.

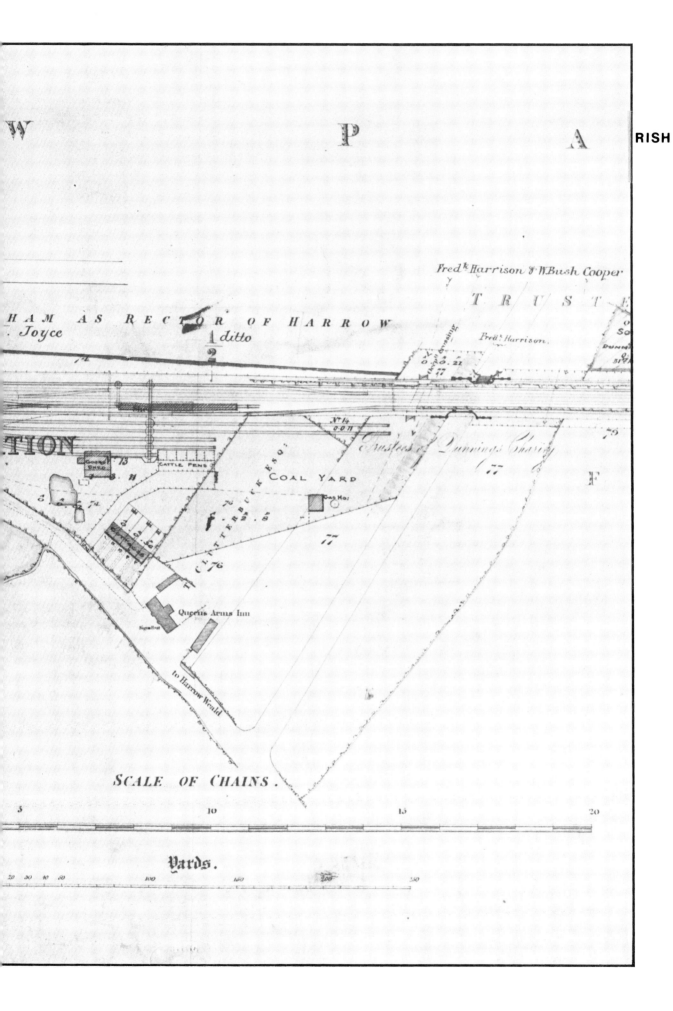

Fred.^k Harrison & W.Bush Cooper

T R U S T E

Fred.^k Harrison.

HAM AS RECTOR OF HARROW
. Joyce

½ ditto

N.º 14
0. 0. 11

Trustees of Dunning's Charity

TION

COAL YARD

Gas Ho:

CATTLE PENS

Queens Arms Inn

to Harrow Weald

SCALE OF CHAINS.

5   10   15   20

Yards.

20 30 40 60   100   150   200   50

nameplates were put up in time for the April, 1871, census, and some roads were renamed. Greenhill Lane, which led from the foot of Harrow Hill, through Greenhill, to Harrow Station, was renamed Station Road. This has caused some confusion in later years as the Metropolitan Railway station, in the heart of Greenhill, is in College Road and not Station Road.

In 1868, a year after the opening of Edgware Station on the Great Northern branch from Seven Sisters Road (now called Finsbury Park), there was a proposal for a link line from Edgware to Harrow (LNWR) Station. This line would have run via Little Stanmore and Stanmore Marsh, but the idea came to nothing. In 1871, however, the proposal was revived as the Harrow, Edgware & London Railway, involving the construction of a line from Greenhill which would again have linked up with the Great Northern Railway at Edgware. Although it was felt desirable to get railway accommodation nearer to Harrow Town than the LNWR station, the roundabout way of getting to London made the scheme unpopular. This, together with the strong opposition which would have been raised by the Great Northern (the proposed line would have become a feeder to the LNWR), caused the death of the undertaking.

On the North Western's main line the long distance traffic to and from the Liverpool Docks and Scotland continued to expand, so the decision was taken to quadruple the tracks from the London end. The LNWR's 1872 Additional Powers Act and 1873 New Works and Additional Powers Act allowed for the quadrupling to take place through the Harrow area. Various small pieces of additional land were acquired and level crossings and footpaths across the tracks were stopped up. (Among the level crossings closed were those at Dirty Lane [now Elmgrove Road], Greenhill — replaced by a subway — and Pinner Park Crossing — traffic diverted via Hatch End Bridge [Headstone Lane], but a footbridge was subsequently provided.)

The fourth line from Primrose Hill through Harrow was ready by 1875. It was laid to the west of the existing three lines, except at Harrow where *two* new tracks were laid on the west side — these became the Down and Up Fast — and the original pair of London & Birmingham railway tracks became the Down and Up Slow. The Up Goods line on the east side of Harrow Station was therefore abandoned, but its approximate alignment was later used by the Harrow & Stanmore Railway to enter the station. All new platforms were provided, and for the first time an entrance to the station was established from Marlborough Road (now called Sandridge Close) on the Greenhill (west) side. The new station building on this side was constructed in a yellow brick Italianate style similar to the existing building on the east side, which was also extended. The footbridge remained in the middle of the station.

The LNWR purchased the land necessary to establish the west-side entrance under their 1872 Additional Powers Act. This land, described as a field, ditch, and plantation and cattle pen, was formerly owned by the Reverend J. W. Cunningham. John William Cunningham had died in 1861, having been Vicar of Harrow for 50 years, and the North Western bought the land from the Reverend F. H. Joyce (Cunningham's successor), Lord Northwick, and the Ecclesiastical Commissioners for England. Marlborough Road was then an unnamed private road over which the LNWR had already obtained a right of way from Station Road (Greenhill Lane) to the station.

In 1880 competition arrived on the scene. The Metropolitan Railway's 'Extension Line', in the guise of the Kingsbury & Harrow Railway, arrived in Greenhill, and also called its station 'Harrow'. The new line was opened on 2nd. August, and provided goods facilities as well. Among those who took advantage of the Metropolitan's arrival were the Harrow Local Board of Health, who established their Materials Depot at Roxborough Bridge, opposite the new goods yard, in order to save cartage from the LNWR station, and the Harrow District Gas Company, who had their coal delivered to the Metropolitan yard, instead of the North Western, as it was nearer to

Two views of the Wealdstone High Street approach to Harrow & Wealdstone Station before the 1910-12 rebuilding. In the lower view (which is from a postcard) the station building is on the extreme right.

Harrow Local History Collection, London Borough of Harrow.

High Street, Station Approach, Wealdstone.

their works at Roxeth. For passengers, however, the omnibus from Harrow Town continued to serve the LNWR station and not the Metropolitan (see Chapter 4).

Another new railway line arrived in 1890, but this time it was a feeder to the LNWR and not in competition with it. The Harrow & Stanmore Railway Company had been incorporated in 1886 and built a line a little over two miles in length from Harrow (LNWR) Station to Great Stanmore (the terminus was, however, simply named 'Stanmore'). The founder and Chairman of the new company was Frederick Gordon, an hotel *entrepreneur*, who had purchased Bentley Priory, Great Stanmore, and turned the mansion into an hotel. He considered that the new branch line would improve communications with his hotel, and he provided most of the capital for the line's construction.

The LNWR carried out a re-arrangement of the tracks at Harrow to accommodate the Harrow & Stanmore Railway for the sum of £1,175. Messrs. Kirk Brothers of Battersea built the new branch platform, most of which was on the Euston side of the road bridge, and the track was on the approximate alignment of the old Up Goods line. A crossover from the branch to the Up Slow line was provided, controlled by Harrow No. 1 signal box (situated where the branch curved away towards Great Stanmore). A run-round loop for the branch locomotive was also provided. The new platform was signed by the Harrow & Stanmore Railway as "HARROW JUNCTION CHANGE FOR L.N.W. RAILWAY". An additional footbridge at the extreme south end of the station was later brought into use, mainly for the benefit of Stanmore passengers.

The new branch line was formally opened by George Findlay, General

A view of Harrow & Wealdstone Station, looking towards Euston, from a postcard franked in 1907. The gas lamps are rather elegant, and have the station name on their globes. LNWR stations were painted brown and buff, and station signs and running-in boards had white cast letters screwed onto a black or dark blue backing.
Courtesy Dilwyn Chambers.

The west-side entrance to Harrow & Wealdstone Station, pictured in January, 1925 (above), and April, 1933 (below). In the lower view, two "LMS EXPRESS PARCELS TRAFFIC" lorries, a cab, and a G.P.O. van await the arrival of the next train.

London Regional Transport.

Manager of the LNWR, at a luncheon held at Bentley Priory on 18th. December, 1890. The first train to Stanmore left Harrow at 12.17 p.m. on that day. The North Western had agreed to operate the line on behalf of the Harrow & Stanmore Railway Company. This arrangement continued until 1899 when the local company was vested into the LNWR and the line (already commonly known as the 'Stanmore Branch') became LNWR property.

The town of Wealdstone had been very slow to develop, but the opening of the Kodak factory to the west of the LNWR main line in 1891 set the pattern for Wealdstone's rapid expansion. Other firms opened factories in and around the town, but it is interesting to note that only Ingall, Parsons, Clive & Company had their factory connected to the railway. A siding from the Stanmore Branch ran into their 'Forward Works' which manufactured coffins.

On 1st. May, 1897, Harrow (LNWR) Station was renamed 'Harrow and Wealdstone' in order to reflect the growth of Wealdstone around the station. Because of the station's position local inhabitants refer to it simply as 'Wealdstone', dropping the Harrow prefix. In 1894 the Metropolitan Railway had confusingly renamed their station 'Harrow *on the Hill*' even though it is in Greenhill and not on the Hill at all.

During 1910 work commenced at Harrow & Wealdstone on the North Western's 'New Line'. This was to be an electric line running from Euston to Watford and providing a much needed suburban service (it is more fully described in Chapter 5). Between Wembley and Bushey the additional pair of tracks for the New Line were to be constructed on the west side of the existing main lines. At Harrow & Wealdstone, however, there was no room on the west side for any new tracks, but there was sufficient space on the east side if the station buildings were rebuilt nearer to the road. It was therefore decided to demolish the east side buildings and slew the Stanmore Branch and the four main line tracks over to the east. This allowed the New Line to use the former Fast line platforms on the west side of the station. The station building on the west side was unaffected by these alterations. The original pair of London & Birmingham tracks now became the Fast lines (see accompanying diagram).

The new station building on the east side was built adjacent to the road (called 'The Bridge') with the passenger entrance facing Wealdstone High Street. Messrs. Higgs & Hill Limited of Crown Works, South Lambeth, signed a standard Building Contract Agreement with the London & North Western Railway Company on 2nd. June, 1910, to build the new station for the sum of £2,890. The Architect was Gerald C. Horsley, FRIBA, of 2, Gray's Inn Square, London, W.C. Horsley was a pupil of Richard Norman Shaw.

The bricks for the new building were "best hard sound square well burnt stocks" and the stonework was in Portland Stone, Granite, and Yorkshire Stone. The Portland Stone above the entrance has the letters "LNWR" carved in it, and the sum of £50 was provided for the carving and £15 for clay models. A doorway (now filled-in) was provided in the flank wall for bicycle and parcels access, and above this doorway is a fine Venetian window which is surmounted by a decorated blank shield. The most noticeable and impressive feature of the station is, however, the orange and white banded clock tower-*cum*-chimney stack which dominates the building. The princely sum of £25 was provided for the clock, fixed complete, and £40 for electric lighting in the new building (an electricity generator was housed in a seperate building between 'The Bridge' and the Stanmore Branch track).

The footbridges in the middle and at the south end of the station were replaced by a new bridge at the north end, costing £2,945 16s. 2d.; half of the bridge is used for parcels and mail which were conveyed to bridge level by lifts from the booking hall and each platform (these lifts have been removed: a conveyor belt now runs from the west side to platforms 2 and 3 only). The new footbridge was built by Messrs. Walter, Scott & Middleton Limited of Westminster, who carried out the work as part of their 'Euston to Watford

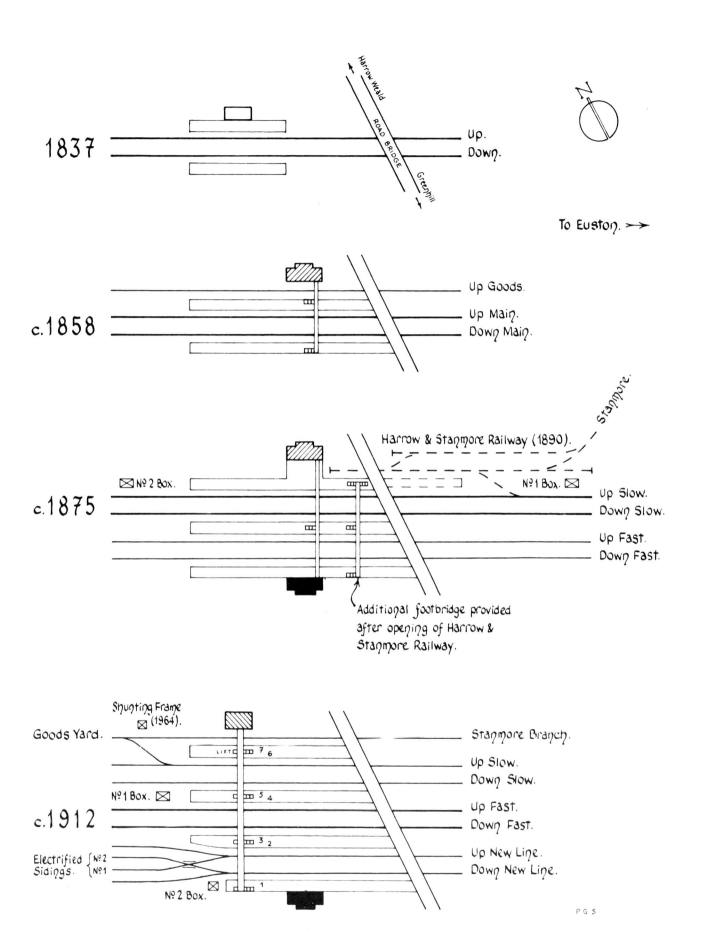

The alignment of the original pair of London & Birmingham Railway tracks is shewn bold throughout. Goods sidings and crossovers between main lines are not shewn as their positions varied considerably over the years.

The Development of Harrow Station.

Additonal Lines' contract. They also built the new platforms, platform buildings, and a fish and milk landing at the north end of the existing west-side building, for the sum of £6,041 3s. 9d. The glazing of the new platform canopies was carried out towards the end of 1911 by Henry Hope & Sons Limited of Birmingham. The 17,430 square feet of "super patent glazing" cost £591 9s. 9d.

The Victorian Society considers that the station is worthy of preservation, but unlike Hatch End Station (also by Gerald Horsley) Harrow & Wealdstone is *not* listed by the Department of the Environment as being of special architectural or historic interest. John Betjeman in his *London Railway Stations* essay commented that Harrow and Pinner (Hatch End) stations were "...in a style half-way between that of a bank and a medium-sized country house. Harrow, with its tower, was remarkably successful".

At the same time that the new station building was being constructed on the east side, the existing building on the west side was refurbished. Alterations costing £904 1s. 0d. were carried out by Messrs. Walter, Scott & Middleton, and on 17th. November, 1910, Messrs. Kirk & Randall of Warren Lane Works, Woolwich, agreed to provide and fix new fittings for the "Parcel and Cloak Room Offices at Harrow Station on the Down Fast [west] Side". The fittings included desks, ticket racks, drawers and cupboards, bicycle racks, and hat and coat rails and hooks in the booking office and Chief Clerk's office. The total cost was £49 7s. 6d. and the work was to be completed within three weeks.

Other alterations on the west side included the cutting-back of the north end of Platform 1 in order to accommodate a new signal box (originally called 'Harrow New Line' but subsequently named 'Harrow No. 2'), and the provision of a reversing siding between the Down and Up New Lines. Soon afterwards a second reversing siding was installed. On the main lines the separate south and north signal boxes (numbered No.1 and No.2

Plan of the new east-side building from The Architectural Review *of September, 1912.*

The Architectural Review.

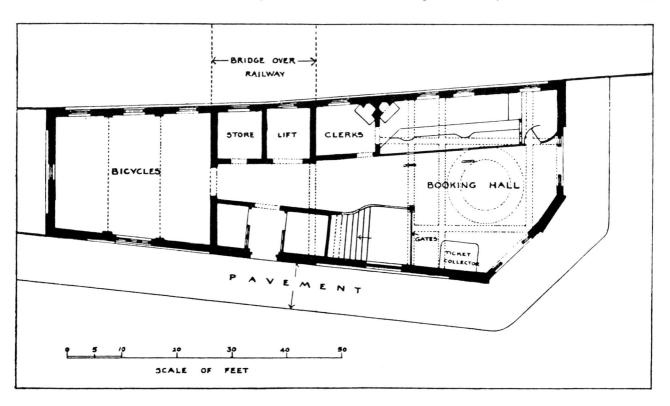

HARROW AND WEALDSTONE STATION (LONDON AND NORTH-WESTERN RAILWAY)
GERALD C. HORSLEY, F.R.I.B.A., ARCHITECT

Harrow & Wealdstone Station on 5th. July, 1911. The new footbridge is in use (although not completed) while the old station buildings on the east side are being demolished to make way for the additional tracks.
Courtesy Hertfordshire Library Service, Watford Libraries.

The old Slow lines at Harrow & Wealdstone on 16th. July, 1911, shortly before they became the Fast lines. Work is in progress on dismantling the middle footbridge and the canopy on the right. The canopy on the left (platforms 2 and 3) remained in position and is still recognizable today. At the time of writing, (May, 1987) the platform buildings on the left are being reconstructed after more than a hundred years in service.
Courtesy Hertfordshire Library Service, Watford Libraries.

respectively) were replaced by a new box at the north end of platforms 4 and 5. This box was named 'Harrow No.1'. The Stanmore Branch was no longer connected to the main line at the south end of the station, and could now only be reached by shunting through the goods yard at the north end. The run-round loop for the branch locomotive was not reinstated in the new track layout as push and pull trains were now operating on this line.

The suburban service over the New Line to Harrow & Wealdstone commenced operation on 15th. June, 1912. However, in the 1912 edition of the *Official Guide to the London & North Western Railway* the emphasis was still very much on the more lucrative long distance traffic. The map of "Anglo-American Routes" in the guide lists 18 towns on its front cover which are in "Direct Connection" with the ports; one of those towns is Harrow. The map itself extends from Winnipeg and Littlerock on the North American Continent across to Harwich and Dover in England, and even the Stanmore Branch is marked. In the same guide the map of "London and Environs" extends no further than North Wembley (a station on the New Line).

The outbreak of the Great War on 4th. August, 1914, delayed the completion of the New Line and, like the Second World War, put the railways under considerable strain. Within days of the Great War being declared a transit camp for troops was established at Harrow Weald. A temporary platform made from railway sleepers was hurriedly erected in the coal yard extension north of Headstone Drive adjacent to Cecil Road. Troops *en route* to Harrow Weald were conveyed to the temporary platform by special trains.

Road transport developed rapidly during the Great War, and, in spite of railway omnibus services and suburban electrification, the railway network never really recovered. The transport policies of successive governments after the Second World War have also contributed to the decline of the most efficient form of transport, the steel wheel on the steel rail. An early casualty in the Harrow area was the Stanmore Village Branch (the 'Village' suffix had

Harrow & Wealdstone east-side building photographed from 'The Bridge' in August, 1950.
London Regional Transport.

The east-side building viewed from Wealdstone High Street in January, 1928 (above), and November, 1930 (below). The rather clumsy-looking wooden boards advertising the train services were erected at most stations along the line in 1929/30. Hardly any two boards had the same wording. By 1950 many of the metal letters had dropped off, and the boards were removed. Note the appearance of the "UNDERGROUND" sign in the lower view.

London Regional Transport.

been added in 1950). On 13th. September, 1952, the last passenger train ran from Harrow & Wealdstone to Stanmore Village. The service had succumbed to competition from buses and the Metropolitan Railway's Stanmore Branch (opened in 1932). Had the LNWR branch been electrified at the same time as the New Line it might well have survived, but the branch was on the opposite side of the main lines and electrification was impracticable. Stanmore Village Goods & Coal Depot remained open for freight trains, and a passenger service continued to operate to Belmont, the intermediate station on the branch, which had opened in 1932 to serve new housing estates.

Just three and a half weeks after the Stanmore closure disaster struck at Harrow & Wealdstone. The second worst accident in the history of British railways occured here on 8th. October, 1952. The sequence of events leading up to the double collision is fully described in Chapter 8. Suffice it to say here that the scars left by the disaster on the station are now unnoticeable, but the scars on the minds of many local people will never be healed.

Harrow & Wealdstone Station looking north from the road bridge in 1912. The New Lines are on the left but are not yet electrified. The signal post, cut off at the top and bottom in this view, is the New Line Up Starter. The LNWR favoured very tall signals in order to give drivers a clear silhouette against the sky, and the signalman a good view of the arm. It was therefore not necessary to provide an electrical repeater in the signal box. A co-acting arm was provided at the driver's eye level.

Locomotive & General Railway Photographs, courtesy David & Charles.

A similar view from the new road bridge in October, 1986. The diamond crossing with a double slip at the entrance to the No. 1 and No. 2 Electrified Sidings can be clearly seen just beyond the footbridge. When the old signalling on the New Line is replaced, the diamond crossing will be removed and only one reversing siding will be provided. There will, however, be an additional crossover between the Down and Up New Lines to the south of the station. Note the running-in board giving passengers a welcome.

Ian Brown.

At the beginning of the 1960's work commenced on the electrification of the main lines through Harrow (see Chapter 9). In connexion with this work, Harrow No.1 Box was closed in 1964, and entry to the goods yard and the Stanmore Village Branch was then controlled by a new signal box called 'Harrow Shunting Frame'. The modest structure was situated next to the branch at the southern end of the goods yard. The A409 road bridge over the lines at Harrow & Wealdstone had to be rebuilt, and a span was provided for the Stanmore Village Branch although it was hardly worthwhile. In July, 1964, Stanmore Village Goods & Coal Depot was closed (it latterly handled only bananas and coal, but the station platform was used to store asbestos cable troughs used in the electrification of the main lines), and on 3rd. October, 1964, the last passenger train ran to Belmont. The branch was a victim of the 'Beeching Axe', and missed-out on electrification for a second time.

With the general decline of wagon-load freight traffic, Harrow & Wealdstone Goods & Coal Depot was closed on 3rd. April, 1967. Towards the end of 1968 the last remaining section of track on the Stanmore Village Branch, 30 chains from Harrow & Wealdstone Goods Yard, through Platform 7, to Christchurch Avenue Bridge, was lifted. This section of line had latterly been used as a headshunt for the goods yard and for testing ballast tamping machines. During 1969 the goods shed at Harrow & Wealdstone was demolished and the goods yard made into a car park. In 1973 the Harrow Shunting Frame was removed.

In 1977 British Rail demolished part of the station building fronting 'The Bridge' because it was "considered to be dangerous". This was the former cycle accomodation which had been disused for some time and was suffering from neglect. The scars left by the demolition were not covered until 1986 when the station received a welcome facelift. A grant of £30,000 from the Greater London Council enabled the cleaning of all the brick and stonework on the exterior of the east side building. Everyone was surprised to find that

the bricks were orange in colour, instead of the dirty red that had become familiar. BR is to spend a similar amount of money in order to improve access for disabled people. It is planned to provide a ramp from the east-side booking hall to Platform 7 (across the trackbed of the Stanmore Village Branch), and a ramped access will also be provided from the west side of the station onto Platform 1.

Harrow & Wealdstone was also one of the first stations to receive a repaint as part of BR's 'Network SouthEast' new image. Station signs have been replaced, and the new running-in boards at the end of the platforms read "Network SouthEast. Welcome to Harrow & Wealdstone". For the first time in many years a good view of the station can be obtained from 'The Bridge' as the wooden buildings and advertisement hoardings between the road and the former Stanmore Village Branch have been removed. It is rather a pity, therefore, that the platform in the foreground (No.7) is bereft of track; a solemn reminder of Dr. Beeching's axing of the branch lines in the 1960's. The station itself, however, is now bright and tidy, and with the efforts of staff and help from passengers will hopefully remain so.

Congratulations, Harrow & Wealdstone, on your 150th. anniversary. In the following chapters we take a look at some of the other aspects of the line's 150 year history...

Gerald Horsley's building now looks a little lop-sided since the demolition of the cycle accommodation. This view was taken in October, 1986, after completion of the refurbishment.

Ian Brown.

The booking hall and clock tower-cum-chimney stack viewed from Platform 5. Most will surely agree with John Betjeman's "remarkably successful" verdict.

Ian Brown.

Below: *An extract from the May 1985 — May 1986 timetable for the New Line in which an error was made in the heading, giving Harrow & Wealdstone Station a slightly more correct name.*

British Rail, London Midland Region.

Table 59
Watford Junction and Wealdstone And Harrow → Queens Park and Euston
Second Class only

Mondays to Fridays

		A		A		A	A	A			A	A	A		A		C		A	C				
Watford Junction ....62, 66 d	0745	....	0757	....	0805	...	...	...	0824	0827	...	...	...	0845	....	0857	...	0905	...	...	0925	...	0945	1005
Watford High Street ....62 d	0748	....	0800	....	0808	...	...	..	0827	0830	...	...	..	0848	..	0900	..	0908	...	...	0928	..	0948	1008
Bushey ....66 d	0751	..	0803	..	0811	...	...	..	0830	0833	...	...	..	0851	..	0903	..	0911	...	...	0931	..	0951	1011
Carpenders Park ....d	0754	..	0806	..	0814	...	...	..	0833	0836	...	...	..	0854	..	0906	..	0914	...	...	0934	..	0954	1014
Hatch End ....d	0756	..	0808	..	0816	...	...	..	0835	0838	...	...	..	0856	..	0908	..	0916	...	...	0936	..	0956	1016
Headstone Lane ....d	0758	..	0810	..	0818	...	...	..	0837	0840	...	...	..	0858	..	0910	..	0918	...	...	0938	..	0958	1018
Harrow & Wealdstone ....66 d	0801	0806	0813	....	0821	...	0827	0836	0840	0843	...	0851	..	0901	0907	0913	...	0921	0927	..	0941	..	1001	1021
Kenton ....d	0803	0808	0815	..	0823	...	0829	0838	0842	0845	..	0853	..	0903	0909	0915	..	0923	0929	..	0943	..	1003	1023
South Kenton ....d	0805	0810	0817	..	0825	...	0831	0840	0844	0847	..	0855	..	0905	0911	0917	..	0925	0931	..	0945	..	1005	1025
North Wembley ....d	0807	0812	0819	..	0827	...	0833	0842	0846	0849	..	0857	..	0907	0913	0919	..	0927	0933	..	0947	..	1007	1027
Wembley Central ....d	0809	0814	0821	..	0829	...	0835	0844	0848	0851	..	0859	..	0909	0915	0921	..	0929	0935	..	0949	..	1009	1029
Stonebridge Park ....d	0812	0816	0824	0826	0832	0835	0837	0846	0851	0854	0856	0901	0908	0912	0917	0924	0927	0932	0937	0944	0952	..	1012	1032
Harlesden ....d	0814	0818	0826	0828	0834	0837	0839	0848	0853	0856	0858	0903	0910	0914	0919	0926	0929	0934	0939	0946	0954	..	1014	1034
Richmond (Surrey) ⊖ 58 d	..	..	0805	...	...	...	..	0825	...	...	..	0845	...	0905	...	...	..	0925	...		0945		1005	
Willesden Jn Low Level ....58 d	0815	0820	0827	0829	0835	0838	0841	0850	0854	0857	0859	0905	0911	0915	0921	0927	0930	0935	0941	0947	0955	..	1015	1035
Kensal Green ....d	0818	0822	0830	0831	0838	0840	0843	0852	0857	0900	0901	0907	0913	0918	0923	0930	0932	0938	0943	0949	0958	..	1018	1038
Queen's Park ⊖ d	0819	0825a	0831	0835a	0839	0844a	0846a	0855a	0858	0901	0905a	0910a	0917a	0919	0926a	0931	0936a	0939	0946a	0952a	0959	..	1019	1039
Kilburn High Road ....d	0821	..	0833	..	0841	...	...	..	0900	0903	...	...	..	0921	..	0933	..	0941	...	...	1001	..	1021	1041
South Hampstead ....d	0823	..	0835	..	0843	...	...	..	0902	0905	...	...	..	0923	..	0935	..	0943	...	...	1003	..	1023	1043
Primrose Hill ....d	..	..	0838	...	...	...	..	..	...	0908	...	...	..	..	..	0938	...	...	...	...	...	..	...	...
Camden Road ....58 d	..	..	0840	...	...	...	..	..	...	0910	...	...	..	..	..	0940	...	...	...	...	...	..	...	...
Caledonian Rd & Barnsbury ....58 d	..	..	0843	...	...	...	..	..	...	0913	...	...	..	..	..	0943	...	...	...	...	...	..	...	...
Highbury & Islington ⊖ 58 d	..	..	0844	...	...	...	..	..	...	0914	...	...	..	..	..	0944	...	...	...	...	...	..	...	...
Canonbury ....58 d	..	..	0846	...	...	...	..	..	...	0916	...	...	..	..	..	0946	...	...	...	...	...	..	...	...
Dalston Junction ....58 d	..	..	0848	...	...	...	..	..	...	0918	...	...	..	..	..	0948	...	...	...	...	...	..	...	...
London Broad Street ⊖ 58 a	..	..	0854	...	...	...	..	..	...	0924	...	...	..	..	..	0954	...	...	...	...	...	..	...	...
Dalston (Kingsland) ....58 d	..	..	..	...	...	...	..	..	...	..	...	...	..	..	..	..	...	...	...	...	...	..	...	...
Stratford Low Level ⊖ 58 d	..	..	..	...	...	...	..	..	...	..	...	...	..	..	..	..	...	...	...	...	...	..	...	...
North Woolwich ....58 a	..	..	..	...	...	...	..	..	...	..	...	...	..	..	..	..	...	...	...	...	...	..	...	...
London Euston ⊖ 66 a	0830	..	..	0848	..	..	0908	..	0928	..	..	0948	..	..	1008	..	1030	1048						

For general notes see front of book

A To Elephant & Castle   C To London Waterloo

Platform 1 at Harrow & Wealdstone in October, 1986. Above is pictured the attractive privately operated 'Jubilee Buffet', and on the left the exit sign mentioning Kodak Works. The flower trolley doubles as a station name sign.
Ian Brown.

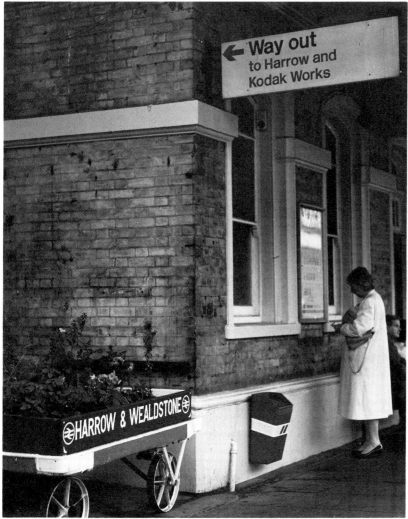

3 THE 'WEST COAST POSTAL'

"Here is a specimen of that exhaustless ingenuity which bids fair to 'annihilate time and space'. That 'time and tide tarry for no man', the dials have long since told us: but the improvement above illustrated [the Travelling Post Office], enables us to work double tides, to duplicate time, and to travel and work at the same instant."

From *The Literary World* (No.35, 23rd. November, 1839).

On 22nd. May, 1838, the first mail trains were operated on the London & Birmingham Railway. These trains consisted of purpose-built sorting carriages, and also included coaches for 1st. class passengers who were conveyed at a premium fare. The section of line between Denbigh Hall and Rugby was not complete at this time, so the *London & Birmingham Railway Post Office* (referred to as the '*Mail*' in timetables) ran between Euston and Denbigh Hall only. The Down departure from Euston was at 8.30 p.m., and the Up departure at 4.00 a.m., on every day of the week (see timetable on page 26).

The idea of a 'travelling post office' had been suggested by Frederick Karstadt, the son of one of the Post Office surveyors. In January, 1838, a temporarily converted horse box was operated as a sorting carriage on the Grand Junction Railway between Birmingham and Liverpool, and it was considered a great success. Rowland Hill had, in fact, mooted the sorting of mails in horse-drawn road vehicles in 1826, but his suggestion was never carried out. The mail trains did not stop at the Intermediate Stations, so any mail for delivery was merely thrown onto the platform as the train passed through. This neither did the letters much good nor the unsuspecting passengers standing on the platform! It became obvious that some form of apparatus would be necessary in order to exchange mail bags with a moving train.

Nathaniel Worsdell, Superintendent of the Grand Junction Railway's carriage works, designed the first exchange apparatus, but the General Post Office failed to agree a price for the use of his invention. John Ramsay, an officer in the G.P.O. Missing Letter Branch, was the next to devise an apparatus. This was successfully tested on the London & Birmingham at Box Moor on 30th. May, 1838. Ramsay's apparatus was installed along the line, but suffered a number of failures in use. Wagon tarpaulins often knocked the mail bags off the post before the travelling post office reached them. John Dicker, an Inspector of Mail Coaches, made a number of modifications, and in 1848 was able to try out his own apparatus. This was accepted by the G.P.O., but it was thought that it might infringe Worsdell's original patent.

The Grand Northern Railroad Post Office *as illustrated in* The Literary World, *23rd. November, 1839.*

Courtesy Railway Gazette.

so its introduction was delayed until 1852 when the patent expired. Dicker's apparatus was to remain in use for nearly 120 years.

With the completion of the London & Birmingham Railway on 17th. September, 1838, London was connected to Birmingham, Liverpool and Manchester by rail, and the opening of the North Union Railway on 21st. October in the same year enabled the *London & Birmingham Railway Post Office* to be extended to Preston on 7th. November, 1838. The new service was named the *Grand Northern Railway [or Railroad] Post Office*. In 1847 this train became the *North Western Travelling Post Office (Day Mail)* and operated between Euston and Perth. Corresponding night services were established at the same time; these are detailed below. The '*Day Mail*' varied its destination over the years, but the service had ceased by 1922.

In 1848 the *Irish Mail* was inaugurated between Euston and Holyhead (for Ireland). Although still running under this name, it is now regarded as a passenger train only, but it does continue to carry 'bagged mails'.

On 1st. July, 1885, a 'special mail' train was inaugurated between Euston and Aberdeen, a distance of 540 miles. The 'special mail' did not have any passenger accommodation, except for a short period when a sleeping saloon and an ordinary carriage were attached on Sundays only "By special arrangement with the Postmaster-General". The *Up Special Mail Travelling Post Office* and the corresponding *Down Special Mail Travelling Post Office* were destined to become the largest travelling post offices in the world.

In 1917 the *Up Special Mail* was amalgamated with the *North Western Travelling Post Office Night Up* (which dated from 8th. May, 1847) and the *Caledonian Travelling Post Office Night Up* (dating from 10th. March, 1848) to form the *Up Special Travelling Post Office* from Aberdeen to Euston. It was not until 1st. September, 1923, that the Down Services were similarly reorganized: the *Down Special Mail* amalgamating with the original *North Western Travelling Post Office Night Down* (8th. May, 1847) and the *Caledonian Travelling Post Office Night Down* (10th. March, 1848) to form the *Down Special Travelling Post Office*, which still left Euston at 8.30 p.m. like the original London & Birmingham Railway mail train. The *Up Special* and *Down Special* are often known as the '*West Coast Postal*' because they take the LNWR/Caledonian Railway West Coast Route to Scotland.

In steam days the '*West Coast Postal*' frequently consisted of fourteen bogie vans, including six sorting vehicles fitted with exchange apparatus. The 40 or so postal workers on board would sort over 150,000 letters on the 11½ hour trip between Euston and Aberdeen. Tremendous mental concentration is necessary as the pigeon-holes are not named but numbered, and the meaning of each number constantly changes as the '*Postal*' progresses along its route.

A carriage print from an original painting by C. Hamilton Ellis entitled "Travel in 1845 — Express mail train of the London & Birmingham Railway". The locomotive is an Edward Bury 2-2-0 No. 32, and the first carriage is the Grand Northern Railroad *travelling post office.*

British Rail, London Midland Region.

The interior of a London & North Western Railway travelling post office. Real Photographs Company, courtesy Ian Allan.

LMS 'Princess Royal' class 4-6-2 No. 6204 Princess Louise *with the* Down Special Travelling Post Office *about to pick-up mail at Harrow & Wealdstone in 1936. Locomotive Publishing Company, courtesy Ian Allan.*

THE 'WEST COAST POSTAL'

Until 1971 mail bags were exchanged at speeds of over 60 m.p.h. by means of the lineside apparatus. A little way south of Harrow & Wealdstone Station there was a pick-up point on the Down Fast line (61 yards before reaching the Outer Home signal), and a set-down point on the Up Fast line (613 yards beyond the platform Starting signal. This greater distance was to allow the mail train to pass through the station before the pouches for despatch were swung-out from the side of the van).

The postal staff on the train had to know exactly where the train was at any given moment. Landmarks, stations, tunnels, and bridges had to be memorized so that the pouches and nets were extended at the right time. Except for the first few exchanges at the beginning of a summer journey, all this was undertaken in the dark. At the trackside the exchange apparatus was marked with a black and yellow chequered plate, and at night a white light was displayed.

To transfer mail to the train, the mail bags were enclosed in stout leather pouches and then mounted on lineside standards. The clearance between a loaded standard and the train was only 1 foot 6 inches, and therefore the heads of the standards were turned away from the track when not in use. Enginemen and guards were warned not to lean out of their trains when passing the exchange apparatus, whether it was in use or not. Each location was provided with a hut for the postmen and a bell worked from the nearest signal box. When the bell rang announcing the approach of the 'Postal' the pouches would be swung out ready to be snatched by the carriage net. The staff on the train had to lower the net in just the right place; too soon and it would hit other lineside structures, too late and the pick-up would be missed. When the net was extended a warning bell rang in the van; this warned postal staff on board to avoid the flying pouches as they arrived at great speed.

To transfer mail from the train to the lineside, the pouches were attached to traductor arms which extended from the side of the carriage. The pouches were suspended about four feet from the ground and three feet from the carriage. On making contact with the ground net the pouches were snatched from the spring-loaded traductor arms which automatically returned inboard.

In addition to the *Up Special* and the *Down Special*, the *North Western Travelling Post Office Night Down* from Euston to Carlisle also passes through Harrow and Wealdstone. This train was inaugurated on 1st. July, 1885, and was originally called the *North Western Travelling Post Office (10 p.m. Mail)*. It received its present title on 12th. July, 1926, and is the second train to run under that name. Other services that ran through Harrow (at the turn of the century) were the *London & Holyhead Travelling Post Office (Canadian Mail)* and the *London & Holyhead Travelling Post Office (U.S.A. Mail)*. The latter ceased operation after the outbreak of the Great War.

Nowadays, mail is no longer exchanged at speed; instead the trains make additional stops at Bletchley, for example, and the *Up Special Travelling Post Office* also stops at Watford Junction. A small despatch of mail is still made from Harrow & Wealdstone, using the 19.28 train to Bletchley, where the mail is transferred to the *Down Special Travelling Post Office*. The last exchange apparatus to be used in normal service was at Penrith, Cumberland, in the early hours of 4th. October, 1971, thus ending a fascinating operation which can, however, still be seen on a couple of preserved lines.

The Down Special Travelling Post Office *catching the mails at Harrow &
Wealdstone in 1947. The string used to keep the pouches steady is just about to be
broken by the carriage net.*

C.R.L. Coles.

*A privately operated horse omnibus on the Bushey Heath — Harrow Station
route pictured outside the east-side entrance to Harrow Station before the 1910-12
rebuilding. The 1892 LNWR timetable shews W.E. Colls operating this service
with two return journeys per day.*
Harrow Local History Collection, London Borough of Harrow.

*The LNWR Pinner Station — Pinner Village horse omnibus in 1914 shortly
before it was replaced by a motor omnibus. The driver is Mr. George Bridge, and
behind him on the roof of the bus is a bag of Royal Mail.*
Harrow Local History Collection, London Borough of Harrow.

4 RAILWAY OMNIBUS SERVICES

"The leading hotel of Harrow is the 'King's Head'. Motor and other omnibuses afford services between the town and the '*North Western*' station, which is supplied with a telegraph office and a bookstall. The Company's motor omnibuses are run from *Harrow Station, via Bushey Heath*, to *Watford*."

From *The Official Guide to the London & North Western Railway*, Eighteenth Edition (Cassell and Company, 1912).

The 1½ mile journey from Harrow Town along the muddy Greenhill Lane to Harrow Station was very inconvenient for the traveller on foot. The King's Head Hotel had the largest stables in Harrow, and it is therefore not surprising that a year or so after the opening of the railway the proprietor of the hotel commenced the operation of a horse omnibus service over these 1½ miles.

The London & Birmingham Railway did not operate any omnibuses itself, but its timetables listed 'Country Coach Proprietors' who undertook to book and deliver parcels for the railway, and also convey passengers and parcels daily to what the railway company termed 'Branch Towns'. In addition to the Harrow Town service, the King's Head is listed in the London & Birmingham's timetables as operating from Harrow Station to the Branch Towns of Pinner and Stanmore. After the opening of Pinner Station, Stanmore was, for a while, regarded as a Branch town from Pinner.

In 1842 the proprietor of the King's Head requested that the London & Birmingham should pay the Duty and License on the Harrow Town omnibus, but the railway company declined to do so. The Coaching & Police Committee stated, however, that they did not want the omnibus to cease running. Of many local routes, including one to Roxeth and services connecting with trains at Sudbury Station, the Harrow Town — Harrow Station route remained in operation for the longest time.

In 1852 the following omnibus services were running to and from Harrow Station: Four return journeys from Harrow Town (operated by James Laws, King's Head Hotel); three return journeys from Bushey (by Joseph Irish); and two return journeys from Great Stanmore (by William Clark) with an additional morning service *to* the station only. At Pinner, Vincent White operated two return journeys from the village to Pinner Station.

A very short-lived service operated for just one month in 1885 from Harrow Town to Harrow (Metropolitan) Station, which had opened in 1880. The LNWR was no doubt thankful that this service was not a success. In September, 1886, the LNWR finally took over the Harrow Town — Harrow (LNWR) Station route from the proprietor of the King's Head, and operated its own horse omnibus. In the previous year the North Western had also started its own service at Pinner which is mentioned below.

The LNWR nearly had to put up with tramway competition in Harrow, for at the turn of the century the Middlesex County Council came up with a number of plans for new tramways. Trams would either skirt the foot of Harrow Hill, or would run over the top of the Hill, and on to Greenhill, Wealdstone, Harrow Weald, and Great Stanmore. Although Greenhill and Wealdstone residents were in favour of the trams, Harrow School and the higher classes on the Hill were very much against them. The Light Railway Commissioners eventually threw out all the tramway proposals, and the trams along the Harrow Road terminated at the Swan Inn, Sudbury, never to progress any further.

It was not until 1906 that the motor omnibus appeared on the scene in Harrow. On 30th. July in that year the LNWR started an ambitious hourly service from Watford Junction to Harrow & Wealdstone Station, running *via* Bushey Station, Bushey Heath, and Harrow Weald. The double-deck Milnes-Daimler buses completed the journey in about 45 minutes for a fare of 8d. The buses stopped anywhere except on the steep hills. The North Western's horse omnibus continued to ply between Harrow & Wealdstone Station and Harrow Town until 12th. July, 1908, when the motor buses from Watford were extended up the Hill to 'Harrow Post Office' (opposite the

King's Head, and not to be confused with the present post office of that name which is in Greenhill).

In September, 1912, the LNWR commenced a local motor bus service between Harrow & Wealdstone Station and Roxborough Bridge *via* Greenhill, and in March, 1913, this route was extended to the Half Moon public house at Roxeth Corner. Later in the same year some buses on this service were diverted at Roxborough Bridge to run along Pinner Road to Bedford Road. On 1st. May, 1914, the Bedford Road service was extended further along Pinner Road to Pinner Village, and then over the LNWR horse omnibus route to Pinner & Hatch End Station.

The North Western's Pinner Station — Pinner Village service ran *via* Paines Lane to the Cocoa Tree Tavern at the top of the High Street, a distance of nearly 1½ miles. This service had been introduced to run in competition with the Metropolitan Railway which had built a station in the centre of the village. Pinner (Metropolitan) Station opened on 25th. May, 1885, and the North Western's horse omnibus to Pinner (LNWR) Station commenced running on the same date. The motor buses did not run along Paines Lane for long as they were soon diverted *via* Pinner Green on roads more suitable for motor traffic.

In July, 1914, the London General Omnibus Company commenced running between Roxeth (South Harrow Station) and Watford, and the LNWR withdrew its Watford Junction — Harrow & Wealdstone Station — Roxeth Corner services. North Western buses continued to operate the Harrow Town and Pinner Station services from Harrow & Wealdstone. Three months later the General service to Watford was withdrawn, and the LNWR resumed its Watford — Harrow & Wealdstone — Roxeth routes as before. The Great War, however, was causing problems as staff were being called-up and vehicles requisitioned, and all LNWR routes in the area were finally withdrawn on 17th. April, 1915.

The London General Omnibus Company eventually covered most of the LNWR routes, but Harrow Town did not see a bus again until the summer of 1966 when London Transport commenced route 136 over the Hill. The 136 serves the Metropolitan station, and not the North Western.

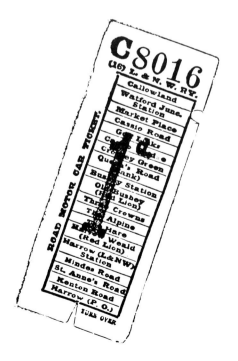

Left: *An LNWR 'Road Motor Car Ticket' for the Callowland — Watford Junction — Croxley Green, and Watford Junction — Harrow Post Office (Harrow Town) routes. (Ticket colour-white.)*

Courtesy John Cummings.

Opposite page (top): *LNWR Milnes-Daimler omnibus No. 8 at Harrow Weald Common on the Watford Junction — Harrow & Wealdstone Station route.*
Real Photographs Company, courtesy Ian Allan.

Opposite page (bottom): *An official LNWR postcard shewing Milnes-Daimler No. 9. The closed-in compartment on the lower deck was for carrying mail bags from Bushey Heath.*

Courtesy Dilwyn Chambers.

On 27th. July, 1906, the Harrow Observer *printed a report of a trial trip on one of the new omnibuses: "There can be no prettier route imaginable than the one chosen, and though the Company have had experience in North Wales and other places, no finer scenery amid country surroundings can be found than at Bushey Heath. It snorted and panted a bit up Clay-hill, and the brakes were a bit hard, but the journey was most enjoyable".*

L. & N.W. MOTOR OMNIBUS RUNNING BETWEEN HARROW & WATFORD VIA BUSHEY HEATH

*Two LNWR Leyland omnibuses outside the west-side entrance to Harrow &
Wealdstone Station, probably during the 1910-12 rebuilding works which closed
the east-side forecourt. The bus on the left is bound for Watford and the one on
the right for Harrow Town.*
Harrow Local History Collection, London Borough of Harrow.

*A London Transport Leyland bus, operating a 'Special Railway Service' due to
Sunday engineering work on the New Line, unloads passengers from the Watford
direction at the west-side entrance to Harrow & Wealdstone on 19th. May, 1985.*
Peter G. Scott.

5 THE 'NEW LINE'

"The latest development of the suburban services running from Euston is supplied by the widening of the lines as far as Bushey for Croxley Green and Watford Junction. This route is now in use as far as HARROW by way of WILLESDEN *(New Station)*, HARLESDEN, STONEBRIDGE PARK, WEMBLEY, NORTH WEMBLEY, and KENTON."

From *The Official Guide to the London & North Western Railway*, Eighteenth Edition (Cassell and Company, 1912).

We have already noted in Chapter 2 that the North Western was not particularly interested in suburban traffic. By the turn of the century, however, suburban traffic was gradually growing in spite of the LNWR. In 1903 the Watford & Edgware Railway Company obtained powers to extend the proposed Hampstead — Edgware tube line on to Watford, and the North Western was forced into action.

In 1907 the LNWR announced that a new electric line was to be built between Euston and Watford alongside the existing main lines (except for a deviation at Watford High Street). At Euston an underground terminal loop would be provided adjacent to the tube stations. In 1909 the LNWR took over the management of the North London Railway, and the electrification scheme was enlarged to include the lines to Broad Street, Kew Bridge, Richmond, and Earl's Court. Also as part of this scheme the London Electric Railway's Bakerloo Line would be extended to Queen's Park (West Kilburn) with through running on to Watford. As the suburban traffic would now be split between three routes at the London end (Euston, Broad Street, and the Bakerloo Line) it was not considered necessary to construct the underground terminal at Euston; the new electric service would use existing surface tracks instead.

The complete scheme was approved in 1911 and was known later as the 'North Western Electric', a title which has now unfortunately been forgotten. It had been decided to press ahead with the construction of the Euston — Watford 'New Line', by which name it was and still is occasionally known, and open it with steam trains as soon as the track and stations were ready. Kenton and Headstone Lane were among five new stations to be initially provided on the New Line, and new platforms were built at the existing stations. At Harrow & Wealdstone the tracks were slewed over, as mentioned in Chapter 2, and here and at Pinner & Hatch End impressive new buildings by Gerald Horsley were erected.

The first section of the New Line to be ready for traffic was that between Willesden Junction (New Station) and Harrow & Wealdstone. The *Daily Graphic* of 3rd. June, 1912, contained an enthusiastic report headed "Railways Moving with the Times — Opening of First Section of a Great Scheme":

"Saturday, June 15th, will be a red-letter day in the history of Harrow. Not only do the King and Queen pay their first visit to the famous school on the Hill, but the Willesden to Harrow section of the London and North Western's new railway will be opened, marking the first stage of a remarkable series of improvements, which will eventually cost £5,000,000...

"What the new line between Harrow and London adds on June 15th. to the present service on the existing lines is as many as 113 trains a day..."

It would have been an even bigger story if King George V and Queen Mary had travelled by train, but nevertheless, the North Western had at long last arrived on the local scene. The *Graphic* further reported that new communities were already springing up along the line, giving Kenton as an example, and concluded:

"The moral of the whole movement is that the London and North Western Company have recognized the call upon them to answer the great expansion of the London suburbs by making further provision for those who have already settled in neighbourhoods served by their

A 'steam navvy' excavator at work on the construction of the New Line.
Courtesy Hertforshire Library Service, Watford Libraries.

Contractors building an additional span to the Dove House Bridge for the New
Line at Pinner & Hatch End. The original London & Birmingham Railway arch
and the station platforms can be seen on the extreme right. This view was taken
on 8th. September, 1911.
Courtesy Hertfordshire Library Service, Watford Libraries.

Erecting steelwork for new platform buildings and canopy at Pinner & Hatch End on 24th. March, 1912. The temporary contractor's track in the left foreground is on the future alignment of the Up New Line.
Courtesy Hertfordshire Library Service, Watford Libraries.

OPENING OF THE NEW LINE
BETWEEN
WILLESDEN AND WATFORD.

Commencing Monday, February 10th, 1913,

many Alterations will be made in the existing Train Services between Watford and Euston, also on the Stanmore, Rickmansworth, and Croxley Green Branches, and regular passengers are requested to carefully peruse the enclosed Time Tables, to prevent disappointment.

Stonebridge Park Station will be closed on Sundays.

For particulars of the running of Horse and Motor Omnibuses see special announcements.

LNWR timetable leaflet for the opening of the New Line to Watford.
Public Record Office, RAIL 981/283.

system. Incidentally, they are drawing new residents out from London to the pleasant places still to be occupied in the seventeen miles between Euston and Watford."

The LNWR even produced a booklet entitled *North Western Country Homes* which extolled the virtues of "London's beautiful North-West".

The steam service over the New Line to Harrow & Wealdstone ran on weekdays only, with trains from Broad Street or Willesden Junction and some irregular trips from Euston. The New Lines were temporarily connected to the main lines at a junction called 'Willesden Tunnel Mouth' which was actually at the west end of the Kensal Green Tunnel.

On 10th. February, 1913, the Harrow & Wealdstone — Watford Junction section of the New Line was ready to receive its steam train service, provided by two-coach push and pull units. The timetable was completely revised,

North-Western Country Homes advertisement from the New Line timetable leaflet.
Public Record Office, RAIL 981/283.

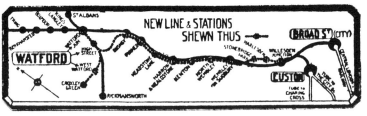

LIVE IN THE COUNTRY.

The Opening of the New L. & N.W. Line between Willesden and Watford on February 10th with

new stations at Harlesden, Stonebridge Park, North Wembley, Kenton, Headstone Lane, Watford West, and Croxley Green, has opened up an entirely new Residential District to the City Man.

This District has been very appropriately called

LONDON'S BEAUTIFUL NORTH-WEST

and, commencing February 10th, the train service from and to Euston will be considerably augmented, making it especially convenient to the City Man.

Cheap Rents.   Perfect Sanitation.   Good Schools.

Excellent Golf Courses.   Ample Water Supply.

Send a post card to Enquiry Office, Euston Station, N.W., for free booklet entitled " North-Western Country Homes."

North-Western Country Homes.

with a daily service from Euston or Willesden Junction and journeys from Broad Street during weekday peak periods.

It was not until 1913 that the LNWR was ready to place the contracts for the electrification of the New Line and the rest of the North Western Electric network. As the new electric lines would connect with the Metropolitan District at Earl's Court Junction, the Metropolitan & Great Western Joint at Uxbridge Road Junction, and the London Electric's Bakerloo Line at Queen's Park, it was obvious that the same method of electrification would be used. This was 630 volts direct current, using 3rd. and 4th. rails.

The Great War inevitably delayed the electrification programme, but on 10th. May, 1915, the Queen's Park (West Kilburn) — Willesden Junction section of the New Line was opened to traffic with a daily service of Bakerloo Line trains. Electrification onwards from Willesden Junction to Watford Junction took place on 16th. April, 1917. On weekdays an all-day service of Bakerloo Line trains was provided plus at peak periods an electric service from Broad Street via Hampstead Heath. Wartime delays with the burrowing junctions at Camden meant that the Euston — Watford Junction peak period service over the New Line continued to be steam operated. There was also one Down steam working from Broad Street on Saturdays. On Sundays the Bakerloo Line trains continued to terminate at Willesden Junction, and the only service forward to Watford Junction was provided by the steam trains from Euston.

A batch of new London & North Western and London Electric Railway joint stock had been ordered for the through Bakerloo Line/New Line

Before the Joint Stock was delivered, the existing Underground stock had an additional step fitted in order to equalize the difference between the LNWR and Bakerloo Line platform heights.
London Regional Transport.

*Motor car No. 3J of the LNW and LER
Joint Stock, photographed in 1920.
London Regional Transport.*

service from Elephant & Castle to Watford Junction, but delivery of this stock was postponed until after the war. Stock therefore had to be borrowed from the Piccadilly Line and the Central London Railway to augment the existing Bakerloo Line cars. The joint stock was eventually delivered in 1920/21. The floors of the cars were 4½ inches higher than ordinary tube stock as a compromise between the different platform heights of the two railways. The cars were lettered 'L&NW AND LER' and painted in North Western colours (the LNWR owned two-thirds of the joint stock). This stock had a very short life as it was replaced in 1930/31 by wholly-owned LER stock. The LMS did retain a few cars for working the Rickmansworth and Croxley Green branches until the outbreak of the Second World War.

For its own exclusive services over the New Line the LNWR provided luxurious saloon cars known as Oerlikon Stock, so named because the electrical equipment was manufactured by Maschinenfabrik Oerlikon of Switzerland. 1st. class accommodation was provided, and the stock was well known for its excellent riding qualities. It was delivered in various stages between 1915 and 1923. (Some earlier Siemens stock had been delivered in 1914 but it was almost exclusively used on the Willesden Junction — Earl's Court service).

During 1919 work on the burrowing junctions at Camden was resumed after the wartime delays. The completion of this work in 1922 enabled the 1911 electrification scheme to be finished at last. On 10th. July, 1922, the full electric service commenced between Euston, Broad Street and Watford Junction, and the steam train service over the New Line was withdrawn.

The 1924/25 British Empire Exhibition at Wembley brought additional traffic to the New Line, and extra trains were operated, including a regular Broad Street — Croxley Green service. After the exhibition finished it was found that most of the additional trains were now needed to cater for the ordinary traffic of the line. The electrification itself had attracted more passengers, and the steady march of houses across the Middlesex fields was attracting even more.

To counteract frequent complaints of overcrowding on the New Line, the

LMS ordered some new stock which commenced operation in 1927. This was known as the G.E.C. Stock, and was built with individual compartments and slam-doors instead of open saloons. This allowed for quicker loading and unloading times. The Oerlikon Stock suffered from long station stops as the motor cars and the control-trailers only had one sliding door on each side of the car. The Oerlikon Stock continued in service, however, and sometimes trains of one set of Oerlikon and one set of G.E.C. stock were formed and nicknamed 'mild and bitter'.

The new stock was in the LMS livery of crimson lake with yellow and black lining, and as the older stock went to Wolverton Works for overhaul the old LNWR livery was over-painted. North Western coaching stock had the distinctive livery of flake white above the waist and alazarine carmine lake below, with lining in yellow and white. A small amount of ultramarine blue was included in the mixture for flake white, but when carriages were freshly varnished the white had a greenish tinge. The alazarine carmine lake was often referred to as 'dark claret' or 'chocolate', and the overall LNWR livery was nicknamed 'plum and spilt milk'.

A further batch of G.E.C. Stock was delivered in 1929, and some trains were lengthened to seven cars. The peak period services on the New Line were now at the maximum that the manual semaphore signalling would allow. The LMS therefore decided to renew the signalling so that the maximum frequency which could be operated along the line would be doubled. The first section to be equipped with the new automatic colour-light signals was between Willesden Junction and Hatch End for Pinner in June, 1932.

Most of the signals were of the three-aspect searchlight type, but had additional marker lights half way down the post. These additional lights were provided to help drivers comply with the 'stop and proceed' rule No.55. If a train arrived at an automatic signal shewing danger (red with a red marker light) a time relay came into operation, and after a prescribed interval the train stop wound down and the marker light changed to yellow, allowing the driver to proceed at extreme caution. This unique signalling system is now being replaced by a modern conventional system costing £2.94 million.

A six-car train of ex-LNWR Oerlikon stock leaves Harrow & Wealdstone en route for Euston in May, 1957. This was the 'Rolls Royce' of electric stock, with mahogany panelling and deep buttoned-in upholstery.

C.R.L. Coles.

THE 'NEW LINE'

The Down New Line Starting signal at Harrow & Wealdstone in October, 1986. The red and yellow marker lights are situated below the telephone 'T' plate. Note the pair of LNWR ground signals (and the pointing hand) controlling the entry to the No. 1 and No. 2 Electrified Sidings. The 'Gap Jumper' is an emergency track-to-train jumper cable which has to be used if a train is 'gapped' (i.e. all shoes of like polarity hanging clear of the conductor rail).

Ian Brown.

In 1933 another batch of G.E.C. Stock entered service and the frequency of trains was increased. The development of the Sudbury Court Estate and the area towards Preston and Woodcock Hill resulted in a new station opening at 'South Kenton' on 3rd. July, 1933.

With the outbreak of the Second World War, service frequencies were reduced, and in 1941 all 1st. class accommodation in the London area was regraded 3rd. class. Seven-car trains were no longer operated, except for a period when prisoners of war were conveyed between Euston and a camp at Headstone Lane.

After the war, service frequencies were gradually increased, reaching a peak in 1949. From 1955 to 1960 the LNWR Oerlikon stock was withdrawn from service, being replaced with new British Railways standard stock which commenced delivery in 1957. From the beginning of the 1960's the services on the whole of the North Western Electric network were gradually reduced, and soon the remaining G.E.C. stock was also withdrawn.

The standard BR livery for electric units was malachite green, which was changed in 1960 to the darker Brunswick green. In 1965 British Railways announced a new 'corporate identity'. For publicity purposes the name was emasculated to 'British Rail' and the double arrow symbol replaced the old 'hot dog' totem. Almost everything that moved had to be painted 'rail blue', and the electric units duly appeared in this rather drab all-over blue livery without any lining. In recent years, however, the former main line livery of pearl grey lined white above the waist and rail blue below was applied to the electric stock as well.

In 1965 the Bakerloo service over the New Line was withdrawn except for four Up trains from Watford Junction in the morning peak and four Down trains in the evening peak. From August, 1970, the North Western Electric network was converted to 3rd. rail operation only, but on sections where the Bakerloo Line trains still operate the 4th. (negative return) rail remains in position and is connected to earth.

After the morning peak on 24th. September, 1982, the Bakerloo service over the New Line was completely withdrawn between Watford Junction and Stonebridge Park (where a new Bakerloo Line Depot had opened). This last reduction in services brought even more protests than usual from the remaining passengers, and accordingly on 4th. June, 1984, a peak service of Bakerloo trains to Harrow & Wealdstone only was reinstated. The Greater London Council also offered financial assistance to BR for the resumption of an off peak weekdays service of Bakerloo Line trains. However, because the G.L.C. was due to be abolished by controversial government legislation on 1st. April, 1986, there could be no guarantee of funding after this date, and BR unfortunately had to refuse the offer. Despite this set-back, it is hoped that an all-day Bakerloo service will return soon. Requests for the Bakerloo trains to be extended to Hatch End have been made, but there are no longer any reversing facilities there (an emergency crossover was formerly provided).

In May, 1985, the New Line's 1957 BR stock (latterly designated class '501') was due to suffer a premature end and be replaced with spare class '313' units from the Great Northern suburban services. Due to a union dispute regarding the maintenance of the '313' units at Hornsey Depot, Eastern Region, the new stock did not replace the '501's until 30th. September, 1985. At times of peak demand the traction supply was inadequate to meet the needs of a six-car '313' set (although there were never such problems with any of the older units), and only three-car trains have been operating with consequent over-crowding. The line voltage has now been increased to 700 volts, so six-car trains could be operated if necessary. The new units are also slightly lighter in weight and often over-ran station platforms until drivers got used to them.

On 20th. November, 1985, the last red train of London Transport Bakerloo Line 1938 stock made its final journey over the New Line in normal service. This train had been restored to its original condition, and occasionally

A three-car train of the new BR Standard stock approaches Kenton Station on the Down New Line on 5th. September, 1957. The two-character headcodes for the New Line, introduced later that month, were as follows: First Character — *B Passenger Train; C Empty Stock.* Second character — *1 Euston/Watford; 2 Broad Street/Watford via Primrose Hill; 4 Broad Street via Hampstead Heath; 6 Willesden New Station; 7 Harrow & Wealdstone; 8 Bushey & Oxhey; 9 Watford/Croxley Green; Y Croxley Green Shed; Z Stonebridge Park Shed.*
British Rail, London Midland Region.

The Monday to Friday through train from Broad Street to Croxley Green arrives at Harrow & Wealdstone on 2nd. June, 1966 (18.22 hrs.). The train — six cars of 1957 stock — is displaying the Bushey & Oxhey headcode. On the following day this through train ran for the last time, and the Colne Junction (Bushey & Oxhey) to Croxley Green Junction spur was then closed. The 'Next Train' indicators on the New Line were manually worked by the platform staff, but with the subsequent demise of such staff many of the indicators are now disused or removed.

Peter G. Scott.

THE 'NEW LINE'

operated enthusiasts' specials. (In the autumn of 1986 four trains of 1938 stock formerly running on the Bakerloo Line were temporarily returned to service to help alleviate overcrowding on the Northern Line.)

The recent success of the London Transport 'Travelcard' prompted the issue of the combined BR and LT 'Capitalcard' based on a similar zonal fare structure, and this is bringing a few more passengers back to the New Line. BR's 'Network SouthEast' promotion, launched on 10th. June, 1986, promises more station staff, a reliable service, and trains in their own distinctive livery of dark grey, red, white and blue. But it will take a lot more than a fresh lick of paint to win back the lost passengers to the New Line which has suffered such a run-down in past years. The stations, however, are already looking brighter, and attractive flower beds have been reinstated on a number of platforms. At Harrow & Wealdstone a couple of redundant platform trolleys are loaded with flowers.

After the last train on Friday, 27th. June, 1986, Broad Street Station was closed, and from the following Monday the few remaining Watford Junction — City trains were diverted to Liverpool Street via a new spur at Graham Road, Hackney. The class '313' units can operate on overhead-wire a.c. as well as 3rd. rail D.C.; the changeover takes place at Dalston (Kingsland) Station for the run 'under the wires' into the Great Eastern's Liverpool Street terminus.

The restored train of 1938 Bakerloo Line stock enters Harrow & Wealdstone Station with an enthusiasts' special on 19th. May, 1985.

Peter G. Scott.

6 THE *ROYAL SCOT* AND OTHER FAMOUS TRAINS

"Over 80 of the most important passenger expresses are named. Some of the names they bear are known all over the world...

"The ROYAL SCOT from London (Euston) to Glasgow takes the West Coast route, via Rugby, Stafford, Crewe, Preston and Lancaster. It crosses the border beyond Carlisle and climbs during its journey the fells of Cumberland and Westmorland and the hills of the Scottish Lowlands."

From *All Along the Line* (British Transport Commission, 1959).

It was always something special to see a 'named train' speeding through a station, with a headboard on the front of the locomotive, and the name of the train (and its destination) repeated on the carriage roof boards along the train's length. The most famous train to run through Harrow & Wealdstone is the *Royal Scot*, which commenced service in 1927 between Euston and Glasgow (with a portion of the train also for Edinburgh).

The history of Anglo-Scottish services actually dates back to 15th. February, 1848, when the Euston — Glasgow service was inaugurated. The journey took 12 hours 10 minutes, but at the commencement of the *Royal Scot* service in 1927 the 401 mile journey was completed in 8 hours 10 minutes. The schedule included a non-stop record breaking run of no less than 299 miles between Euston and Carlisle. The LMS introduced new classes of locomotives to work its prestige trains, these were the 'Royal Scot', the 'Princess Royal', and the 'Princess Coronation' types. Some of the 'Princess Coronation' locomotives were streamlined in order to reduce wind resistance.

In 1937 the LMS introduced its first fully streamlined train to mark the Coronation of King George VI and Queen Elizabeth. It was called the *Coronation Scot* and ran between Euston and Glasgow in 6½ hours. The service was withdrawn in 1939 on the outbreak of the Second World War. The war also put an end to the rivalry between the LMS West Coast Route and the LNER East Coast Route for the fastest service to Scotland.

The *Royal Scot's* journey time had been reduced to seven hours by 1939, but diesel haulage in the post war years brought little further acceleration. The writer, as a small boy, remembers making a special journey to Kenton Recreation Ground to see the LMS diesels Nos. 10000 and 10001 roar through with the *Royal Scot* a little after 10 o'clock: diesel locomotives were a novelty then. On the completion of the Euston — Glasgow electrification in 1974 the journey time was reduced to five hours at an average speed of 80 m.p.h. In July, 1987, the *Royal Scot Limited* (the suffix was added in May, 1987) celebrates its Diamond Jubilee, and it will hopefully continue to be the foremost train on the West Coast Route for many years to come.

Another famous named train to run through Harrow & Wealdstone is the *Irish Mail* (mentioned in Chapter 3). This train first ran from Euston to Holyhead on 1st. August, 1848, and is the oldest named train in the world. Of the North Western's other named trains to pass through Harrow the *Sunny South Express* is one of the best remembered. It ran for many years and continued well into LMS days, until the Second World War. This train provided a through service from Liverpool, Manchester, and Birmingham to Brighton and Eastbourne via Willesden Junction, Kensington (Addison Road), and Clapham Junction. In 1986 British Rail re-introduced through services from the North-West to the South-East of England via Kensington (Olympia) (renamed in 1946) but the *Sunny South Express* name has not, as yet, been revived. Another well known North Western train was the 2.00 p.m. Scotch Dining-car Express, always known as the '*Corridor*' after the introduction of corridor coaches in 1893. It was the fore-runner of the *Midday Scot*.

At the end of the 1950's seventeen named trains were running through Harrow & Wealdstone. In addition to the *Royal Scot* and the *Irish Mail* there were the following:

The Red Rose	- Liverpool
The Merseyside Express	- Liverpool

LONDON AND MANCHESTER	IN 4¼ HOURS.
LONDON AND LIVERPOOL	IN 4½ HOURS.
LONDON AND BIRMINGHAM	IN 2½ HOURS.
LONDON AND EDINBURGH	IN 8½ HOURS.
LONDON AND GLASGOW	IN 8¾ HOURS.
LONDON AND CHESTER	IN 4 HOURS.
LONDON AND ABERDEEN	IN 12¼ HOURS.

SLEEPING SALOONS ON THE NIGHT TRAINS.

Journey times from Euston, as displayed on the cover of the December 1892 LNWR timetable.

Peter G. Scott's collection.

The Down Sunny South Express *approaching Kenton in 1913, headed by LNWR 'Precedent' class 2-4-0 No. 514 Puck and 'Jubilee' class 4-4-0 No. 1926 La France.*
Locomotive & General Railway Photographs, courtesy David & Charles.

The Mid-day Scot	- Glasgow
The Shamrock	- Liverpool for Ireland
The Mancunian	- Manchester
The Comet	- Manchester
The Ulster Express	- Heysham for Belfast
The Lakes Express	- Windermere and Workington
The Welshman	- Portmadoc and North Wales resorts
The Midlander	- Birmingham
The Manxman	- Liverpool for the Isle and Man
The Northern Irishman	- Stranraer for Larne and Belfast.
The Caledonian	- Glasgow
The Royal Highlander	- Inverness
The Lancastrian	- Manchester

The 1970's saw a marked decline in the number of named trains, but there has been a recent revival and the summer 1987 timetable shews the following running through Harrow & Wealdstone:

The Birmingham Pullman (UP only.)	- Birmingham New Street
The Manchester Pullman (*3 journeys*.)	- Manchester Piccadilly
The Merseyside Pullman (*3 journeys*.)	- Liverpool Lime Street
The Clansman	- Inverness
The Irish Mail (*2 journeys*.)	- Holyhead for Dun Laoghaire
The Royal Scot Limited	- Glasgow Central
The Cambrian Coast Express	- Aberystwyth (Pwllheli on Fridays)
The Welsh Dragon/Y Ddraig Gymreig	- Holyhead and North Wales resorts
The Lancashire Pullman	- Blackpool North
The West Midlands Executive	- Shrewsbury
The Royal Highlander	- Inverness
The Nightrider	- Glasgow Central
The Night Limited	- Glasgow Central and Perth
The Night Scotsman	- Edinburgh

Headboards are now rarely carried, and carriage roof boards are a thing of the past, so today's named trains run somewhat anonymously, which is a pity.

LMS 'Princess Coronation' class 4-6-2 No. 6229 Duchess of Hamilton, *masquerading as No. 6220* Coronation, *passing South Kenton with the* Coronation Scot *streamlined train on a test run in January, 1939. Later that month the locomotive and train were shipped to the New York World's Fair, hence the headlamp to comply with American practice.* Duchess of Hamilton *was preserved by Butlins Ltd. at their Minehead holiday camp, but is now in the custody of the National Railway Museum at York. The* Duchess *(without her streamline casing since 1948) has recently been operating through the Borough of Harrow again, on the summer Sundays steam hauled Marylebone — Stratford-upon-Avon train which passes through Sudbury Hill, Harrow, on the Great Central line.*

C.R.L. Coles.

THE ROYAL SCOT
LONDON (EUSTON) — GLASGOW

In 1950, British Railways designed new carriage roof boards for the Royal Scot *train in Stuart Royal tartan.*

British Rail, London Midland Region.

Ex-LMS 'Princess Royal' class 4-6-2 No. 46201 Princess Elizabeth *with the Down* Mid-day Scot *north of Hatch End on 6th. August, 1953.*

British Rail, London Midland Region.

The Down Royal Scot, *running on the Slow line, passes track relaying work near Hatch End on 22nd. October, 1961. The locomotive is a diesel-electric of the D200 series.*

British Rail, London Midland Region.

The Down Midlander *bound for Birmingham passes through the original London & Birmingham Railway arch (supplemented by a girder span) at Harrow & Wealdstone in 1951. The locomotive is an ex-LMS 'Jubilee' class 4-6-0 No. 45738* Samson.

C.R.L. Coles.

The Up Midlander *running through Harrow & Wealdstone in March, 1952, hauled by another 'Jubilee', No. 45734* Meteor.

C.R.L. Coles.

79

Two views of the Down Red Rose *Liverpool train passing through Harrow & Wealdstone. Above, ex-LMS diesel-electric No. 10000 enters the station in June, 1952, and below, the rear end (not the same train!) pictured as it leaves the station.*
C.R.L. Coles.

7 A TRAIN RIDE THROUGH HARROW

"Resuming our journey towards the picturesque countryside of 'Greater London', we now move onwards to SUDBURY AND WEMBLEY. Farther distant we may discern the fine mansion of Bentley Priory, while as we approach the HARROW AND WEALDSTONE station to the left rise the wooded heights of HARROW."

From *The Official Guide to the London & North Western Railway*, Eighteenth Edition (Cassell and Company, 1912).

Since the development of the early coach roads travellers have wanted to know which towns they were passing through and what time they were likely to arrive. The coming of the railways provided an even greater opportunity for travel, and the demand for 'Railway Guides' was soon met by enterprising publishers. These guides usually gave a description of the route and the surrounding countryside, often with a map and sketches of landmarks, and also included a copy of the timetable with fares appended.

The railway guides soon developed into separate publications for the description of the route and for the timetables, as the latter altered frequently. *Bradshaw's* famous timetables were first published in 1839, and over the years most main line railway companies published descriptive guides for their most popular routes. The LNWR published a volume covering the whole of its network, and latterly running to some 600 pages. Even today British Rail still occasionally publishes route leaflets, although it is now virtually impossible to read station names as the speed of trains gets faster and faster.

For our 'Train Ride Through Harrow' we will go back to the still somewhat leisurely LMS days. We commence our journey early in the morning at Watford Junction Station, and armed with a copy of *LMS Route Book No.2* (see Bibliography) board a main line train for the run to Euston. On the following pages the straight-line map (to the scale of half an inch to the mile) is reproduced, and is followed by the detailed description of the journey:

An Up Northampton — Euston semi-fast train approaching the Pinner Park Crossing footbridge in 1938 with ex-LNWR 'Prince of Wales' class 4-6-0 No. 25673 Lusitania.

C.R.L. Coles.

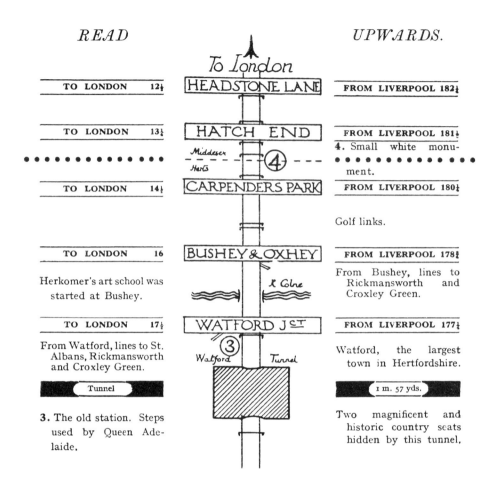

TO LONDON 12½	FROM LIVERPOOL 182¼
TO LONDON 13½	FROM LIVERPOOL 181¼
	4. Small white monu-ment.
TO LONDON 14½	FROM LIVERPOOL 180½
	Golf links.
TO LONDON 16	FROM LIVERPOOL 178¾
Herkomer's art school was started at Bushey.	From Bushey, lines to Rickmansworth and Croxley Green.
TO LONDON 17½	FROM LIVERPOOL 177½
From Watford, lines to St. Albans, Rickmansworth and Croxley Green.	Watford, the largest town in Hertfordshire.
Tunnel	1 m. 57 yds.
3. The old station. Steps used by Queen Ade-laide.	Two magnificent and historic country seats hidden by this tunnel.

All bridges *over* the line **except** footbridges are shown, to aid in identifying places and views.

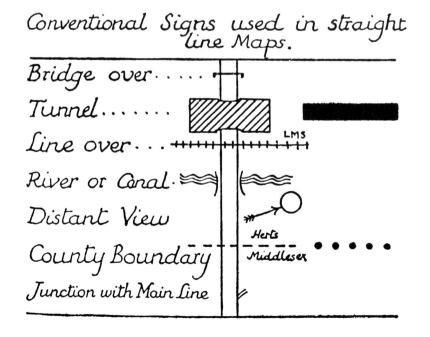

Conventional Signs used in straight line Maps.

Bridge over ·····
Tunnel ·······
Line over ···
River or Canal ·
Distant View
County Boundary
Junction with Main Line

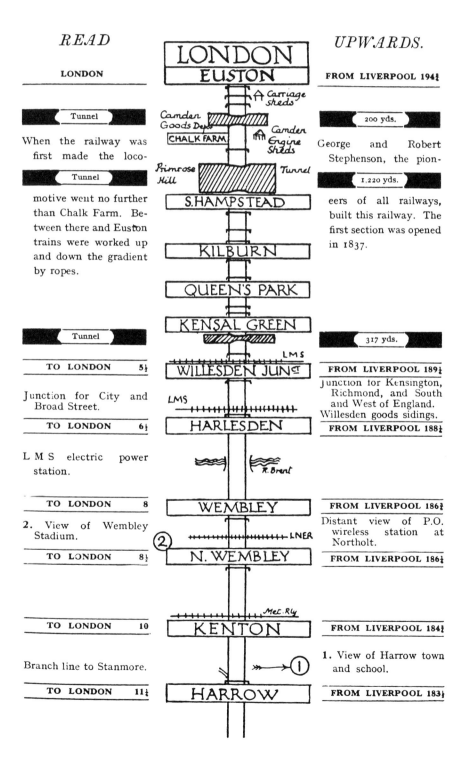

LONDON

Tunnel

When the railway was first made the loco-

Tunnel

motive went no further than Chalk Farm. Between there and Euston trains were worked up and down the gradient by ropes.

Tunnel

TO LONDON   5½

Junction for City and Broad Street.

TO LONDON   6½

L M S electric power station.

TO LONDON   8

2. View of Wembley Stadium.

TO LONDON   8½

TO LONDON   10

Branch line to Stanmore.

TO LONDON   11½

FROM LIVERPOOL 194½

200 yds.

George and Robert Stephenson, the pion-

1,220 yds.

eers of all railways, built this railway. The first section was opened in 1837.

317 yds.

FROM LIVERPOOL 189½

Junction for Kensington, Richmond, and South and West of England. Willesden goods sidings.

FROM LIVERPOOL 188½

FROM LIVERPOOL 186¾

Distant view of P.O. wireless station at Northolt.

FROM LIVERPOOL 186¼

FROM LIVERPOOL 184½

1. View of Harrow town and school.

FROM LIVERPOOL 183½

LONDON
EUSTON

Camden Goods Depot
CHALK FARM
Camden Engine Sheds

Primrose Hill — Tunnel

S. HAMPSTEAD

KILBURN

QUEEN'S PARK

KENSAL GREEN

WILLESDEN JUNCᵗ

HARLESDEN

R. Brent

WEMBLEY

N. WEMBLEY

KENTON

HARROW

A TRAIN RIDE THROUGH HARROW

And here follows the detailed description of the journey from the *LMS Route Book* (by kind permission of British Rail, London Midland Region) which we pick up on the approach to Bushey & Oxhey:

Crossing the River Colne on a viaduct we come to Bushey. It was here that the great painter Herkomer established his school of art which made its influence felt far and wide. The school still continues as a private institution.

CARPENDERS PARK
HATCH END

The junction of Hertfordshire and Middlesex is marked by a white pillar set up on the right-hand side between Carpenders Park and Hatch End Stations. It has on it the arms of London and the somewhat cryptic inscription 'Act 24 & 25 Vict. Cap 42'. This refers to the London Coal and Wine Duties Act of 1861 and signified in its day that any wine, coal, or cinders — a strange category — passing this post were subject to a duty levied by the Corporation of London.

HARROW

The hill of Harrow now becomes conspicuous on the right hand, crowned by its town and famous public school. Rising above the flat plain with its trees and spires and buildings, it cuts a striking figure in the green landscape like an island of romance. Among famous old Harrovians were Sir Robert Peel, Lord Byron, and Lord Palmerston. The taller spire is the parish church, the lesser the school chapel by Sir Gilbert Scott. In the churchyard is an epitaph to an engine driver who was killed in 1838, the first year the line was open from London to Birmingham. It must have seemed a specially horrible death to be run over by one of those fierce, primitive, monster-novelty locomotives. The epitaph is gruesome and befitting the experience. It begins pitifully:*

To the Memory of
THOMAS PORT
SON OF JOHN PORT OF BURTON UPON TRENT
IN THE COUNTY OF STAFFORD, HAT MANUFACTURER,
WHO NEAR THIS TOWN, HAD BOTH HIS LEGS
SEVERED FROM HIS BODY BY THE *RAILWAY TRAIN.*
WITH THE GREATEST FORTITUDE HE BORE A
SECOND AMPUTATION BY THE SURGEONS, AND
DIED FROM LOSS OF BLOOD.
AUGUST 7TH, 1838, AGED 33 YEARS.

Bright rose the morn and vig'rous' rose poor *Port*;
Gay on the *Train*, he used his wonted sport:
Ere noon arrived his mangled form they bore,
With pain distorted and o'erwhelm'd with gore;
When evening came, to close the fatal day,
A mutilated corpse the sufferer lay.

In those days (being prior to 1845) the law of deodand had not been abolished, and by its ancient usage the instrument of accidental death — in this case a steam engine — was liable to punishment by a fine or its equivalent value being forfeit to the King, who was

The coal duty pillar on the Hertfordshire/Middlesex county boundary, as pictured in the LMS Route Book. *It is still in position, but is now very rusty.*
Courtesy British Rail, London Midland Region.

* The *LMS Route Book* only quoted the first two lines of the verse, but here the full inscription on the gravestone is given. The grave is by the church tower.

A TRAIN RIDE THROUGH HARROW

NORTH WEMBLEY

supposed to put the money to pious uses.

Passing North Wembley, the Stadium and buildings of the British Empire Exhibition of 1924-25 come well into view on the left hand.

The wireless masts that appear to the South of Harrow Hill belong to the Government radio station at Northolt.

The LMS generating station for supplying electric power to the railway on the suburban section has architectural distinction. We pass it on the left after Wembley Station. Then, crossing the Brent, a tributary of the Thames (almost obscured by the number of bridges that span it at the one place), we run through a long zone of sidings into Willesden Junction. Willesden is a junction for the City, Kensington, and Richmond. The bye-pass line *via* Chelsea to the South of England turns off here. The town is ancient. Its parish church possesses several fine brasses and there are relics of Norman masonry in its fabric.

WILLESDEN

Through the suburbs of North-west London we go, and after South Hampstead Station run under Primrose Hill in a tunnel. On the far side we pass outside Chalk Farm Station and the great goods depot of Camden Town beyond. In early days the locomotive was unhooked here, as at Edge Hill, and the train was lowered down the gradient into Euston Station, a gradient that the modern express engine can take at the gallop with a heavy train. Thus we come to the end of our journey.

EUSTON

Having safely reached Euston we must hurry across to Platform 13 where the *Royal Scot* will depart at 10 o'clock. Our return ride through Harrow will be far more exciting, as we have a 'footplate pass' that will enable us to travel in the cab of the locomotive.

At the far end of the platform we find No.6206, an LMS 'Princess Royal' class 4-6-2 locomotive named *Princess Marie Louise*. We join Driver L.A. Earl by the engine, and he will describe the run from Euston for us:*

Well, it is nearly ten o'clock. The passengers are inside the train and are leaning out of the carriage windows, bidding their friends good-bye, the doors are closed, the diminished group by the engine has moved back a little, away from the platform edge; the inspector is glancing searchingly along the train to make sure that all is well, the locomotive's fire is roaring away merrily, and the engine is emitting a deep, sonorous murmur, seemingly impatient to start on its race against the clock. We must be up on the foot-plate and ready for action; my fireman is there, attending to injectors and arranging fire-irons....

The hands of the big station timepiece point to exactly ten o'clock. The starting-signal is 'off'. The guard is blowing his whistle and waving his green flag. I reply with a piercing note from my engine whistle, ease open the regulator, and take my stand by my lookout window.

Like a giant greyhound freed from the leash, our powerful No.6206 glides forward with its 420-ton train, to the accompaniment of quickening bursts of exhaust from the chimney.

Good-bye, London; we are off to Carlisle!

* This description is taken from *Speeding North With The 'Royal Scot' — a Day in the Life of a Locomotive Man* by Driver L.A. Earl (in collaboration with H. N. Greenleaf) by kind permission of the Oxford University Press. In this account, the Fast and Slow lines are referred to as 'Through' and 'Local'.

A TRAIN RIDE THROUGH HARROW

Over the points we go, on to the Down Through Road. My fireman (his name is Tom) picks up his shovel and commences stoking. I adjust the reversing-wheel, so that the pistons receive a good pressure of steam, and take my stand in front of my look-out window. The beat of the pistons and the exhaust from the chimney are making a nice rhythmic sound as No.6206 gets into its stride. 'Sh-sh-sh-sh', 'sh-sh-sh-sh', 'sh-sh-sh-sh', it seems to say, as it gathers speed.

The Distant, Home, and Starting Signals are all 'off', so we can forge ahead. Tom admits water to the boiler by opening an injector steam valve and works the water-regulator valve....

We are no sooner out of Euston than we pass through a short tunnel which we call Park Street Bridge. I pull the whistle lever. There is a loud shriek and we plunge inside, clouds of smoke and steam enveloping us and some of it finding its way into the cab. The tunnel is only 166 yards long and we are soon out again into the open.

On our left now is the Camden Locomotive Depot, at which we arrived a short time ago, and on our right is the big LMS Goods Depot of the same name. We have been climbing steeply since we started — a 1 in 70 gradient — but No.6206, putting forth its utmost power, has breasted this slope without complaint.

Another tunnel looms ahead — a long one, Primrose Hill, 1,182 yards. I pull the whistle lever as we enter with a rush. Smoke and steam are all around us once more, and I sound the whistle half way through, and again at the exit, to warn any men who may be working just outside of our approach. Tom opens the 'blower' as we enter to maintain a good draught for the fire, but closes it as we emerge.

A local train for London passes as we run easily through Queen's Park Station, 3½ miles from Euston. The signals which govern our track are all pointing downwards, and our road is clear...

Tom has left off firing for a moment and is breaking coal with a hammer. I pull the whistle lever as we plunge into Kensal Green Tunnel, 320 yards long. Tom again opens and closes the blower and resumes his labours with the shovel as we rush through Willesden. I again sound the whistle; a prolonged note this time. We have covered 5½ miles in 9 minutes, and the engine is warming up to its work. We pass the Willesden Goods Sidings and the dingy roof-tops of London at 55 miles an hour.

Tom grasps a brush with which he sweeps the floor, afterwards spraying it with water to lay the dust. In the course of firing pieces of coal inevitably fall on the floor, but they cannot be allowed to remain there. The foot-plate must be kept clean, and besides, the fireman might twist his ankle if he stepped on some pieces of coal.

We flash through Wembley and I adjust the reversing-lever to 20 per cent. of the pistons' travel, taking full advantage of the steam's expanding qualities, and am now sitting on the little seat provided for me, intently watching the signals. Although there is a window — which some of us drivers call a 'weather-glass' — immediately in front of me, I prefer to look out through the open window in the side of the cab. I do not catch the draught, however, because my face is shielded by a glass screen about 5 inches wide. We pass a Post Office ground apparatus, with its yellow-and-black squared warning-board, and Tom is firing again. We have left behind the dingy London roof-tops and are now in the region of trim suburban villas, each with its neat little garden. Away to the right can be seen the buildings of the famous Wembley Stadium, and as we rush under a bridge a familiar red motor-bus nonchalantly passes over the top.

The groundsman of a large playing-field is complacently rolling a cricket-pitch, but a freight train travelling in the opposite direction passes us at this moment and blots out that picture.

With a deafening roar a quantity of steam escapes from the safety-

A TRAIN RIDE THROUGH HARROW

valves, fitted on top of the boiler just in front of the cab. This means that the full steam pressure of 250 lb. per square inch has been reached; in other words, the boiler is making steam faster than the engine is using it. The steam escape ceases as we rush through Harrow, 11¼ miles from London. I sound the whistle to warn some permanent way men who are walking along the track, carrying sleepers, then glance at the boiler water-gauge glass to note the level of water in the boiler.

The famous Public School, founded by John Lyon in 1571, is away to the left, and another 'chess-board' indicates Post Office ground apparatus.

Hatch End, 13½ miles: Tom has laid aside his shovel and is adjusting the water regulator for the injector.

A Euston-bound express flashes past us, and a freight train, also going towards London, rolls along on the Up Local line. I adjust the reversing-wheel to 18 per cent., and Tom resumes firing.

We overtake an Underground electric train that has recently emerged from the bowels of the earth, and is heading for Watford. How diminutive it looks! It seems a mere toy by comparison with our giant engine and thirteen roomy carriages. No sooner are we past this than we rush by a freight train on the Down Local line, and at the same time an express roars between the freight and ourselves on the Up Through.

We have just crossed the boundary between Middlesex and Hertfordshire, and are rapidly approaching Bushey and Oxhey Station, 16 miles from Euston. This is where the pretty country really begins. Hertfordshire is noted for its landscapes, and the beautiful park-like scenery, so restful and quiet, is a joy to behold. Soft meadow-land, with cows grazing placidly here and there, gentle hills covered with trees, a golf course, a farm — it is all so typically English.

We have just come over a water-trough and passed another northward-bound train on the Down Local line. I indicated to Tom by a shake of the head that I did not want him to use the scoop. We have enough water in our tender at present and need not pick up any more until we reach Castlethorpe. Tom has adjusted the damper to the fire-grate by manipulating a lever on the floor, and is looking through his window watching the smoke from our chimney. Why is he doing this? Because while the chimney is smoking well he knows that the fire is burning properly; directly the smoke diminishes it means that some portion of the grate has become uncovered and air is getting through. More coal therefore has to be piled on to the fire.

Fire will not burn without air, as you probably know. On a locomotive a fire-hole door and a 'damper' are fitted so that the right quantity of air can be admitted to the engine's fire. The correct use of the door and the damper ensure that the fuel will be completely consumed, thereby providing the maximum amount of heat. Otherwise coal is wasted through unburned particles being drawn through the smoke tubes and nasty black smoke is emitted from the chimney, which is a nuisance. When the fire is burning properly the temperature in the fire-box is something like 2,500 degrees Fahrenheit.

Beautiful big rolls of steam and smoke are driving over us now; but as we roar over the River Colne — which joins the Thames near Staines — Tom again gets to work with his shovel. He cannot rest more than a few minutes at a time because the fire must be kept burning fiercely during the whole of the journey, otherwise we should not be able to maintain our steam pressure.

I see colour-light signals ahead, showing a green aspect, and several cross-over roads. Watford. I give a very long whistle as we flash through the station. Many people are on the various platforms, and they gaze at our engine and train in admiration as we tear by.

Another Post Office 'chess-board'. We are now really travelling. We

have covered 17½ miles in 21 minutes, and our speedometer indicates more than 60 miles an hour. There is a fine wholesome noise in the cab; a sound composed of swiftly moving pistons, a roaring fire, the rapid clang of connecting-rods and coupling-rods outside, and the good metallic ring of 160 tons of steel passing over steel rails. You cannot hear yourself speak; but then, you do not have to speak. Engine drivers and firemen are far too busy at their respective jobs to converse with each other; and there is plenty of time for conversation at the end of the journey.

There is a black, yawning gap ahead. It is the entrance to Watford Tunnel. I give a long whistle as we rush inside, and Tom manipulates the blower again. The glare from our open fire-box illuminates the surrounding darkness. The tunnel is 1 mile 57 yards long, but the speck of light at the far end comes rapidly nearer; in a flash we are out in the open again; we have passed through in 45 seconds, and are now running alongside the Grand Junction Canal, which before the era of railways was the main artery of inland navigation between the north of England and London...

...And so the *Royal Scot* speeds on to its first stop at Carlisle, but we must leave Driver Earl's travelogue here before we get carried away too far!

The Down Royal Scot *on Bushey Troughs hauled by LMS 'Royal Scot' class 4-6-0 No. 6111* Royal Fusilier *in 1933.*

C.R.L. Coles.

8 ACCIDENTS WILL HAPPEN . . .

"...suddenly — just as they were nearing Harrow — there was a terrific crash — a catastrophe never to be forgotten. The express had run into an obstruction in front, and Harrow Station was turned into an accident ward filled with the moans of the wounded and the murmurs of the dying."

From " 'Snatch': A Railway Story", in *The New Penny Magazine* (Vol.II, 1899).

Mention "accident" and "Harrow & Wealdstone" in the same breath and thoughts will probably immediately turn to the disaster that occurred in 1952. It is not generally known, however, that this was the third major accident at Harrow Station, although the previous two did not involve such a terrible loss of life.

The first accident happened just three years after the line had opened, on 12th. November, 1840. The 10.00 a.m. merchandise train from Birmingham suffered a broken wagon axle at Woodcock Hill (mid-way between the present Kenton and South Kenton stations) and the train had become derailed. A primitive form of 'single line working' was introduced, with all traffic using the unblocked Down line. These arrangements were in the hands of the London & Birmingham's Superintendent of Police (as mentioned in the Introduction, signalmen were originally called policemen).

A light engine from Tring arrived at Harrow at about 2.30 p.m., soon after the derailment had occurred. Driver Bradburn and Fireman Finch were on the footplate of this locomotive, No.15, and they were instructed to run between Harrow Station and the derailment at Woodcock Hill to convey messsages associated with the single line working. No.15 ran to and fro on the blocked Up line, while arrangements had been made for all Up trains to Euston to cross over onto the Down line at Harrow.

Before 6.00 p.m. No.15 was sent from Woodcock Hill to Harrow with the instruction that all Up trains should be held until the 6 o'clock Down train had passed. Driver Bradburn had also been requested to order refreshments for the men working at Woodcock Hill from the Queen's Arms public house, close to Harrow Station. Bradburn left his engine on the Up line in charge of Fireman Finch, telling him that if an Up train approached he should move the engine towards London out of its way. Although London & Birmingham Railway passenger trains ran to a timetable, the goods trains did not, so it was impossible to tell when the next train would be expected.

No sooner had Driver Bradburn left the station forecourt to go to the Queen's Arms than he heard the sound of an approaching train on the Up line. He ran back to the station and saw that Finch was moving No.15 along the line as instructed. Fireman Finch, however, soon realized that the approaching train, a double-headed goods, was not going to stop, even though it had been shewn a red light by the policeman on approaching the station. Finch shut off steam and jumped from No.15.

The pilot (leading) engine of the goods train was No.1, which had just been repaired at Wolverton Works, and the train engine was No.82. In the resulting collision Fireman Dawson on No.1 and Driver Simpson on No.82 were killed. It transpired at the Coroner's inquiry that Simpson was a somewhat reckless driver. At the moment of impact his engine was still running with full steam in forward gear, but No.1 had been put in reverse gear and the fireman was putting on the brake. Although killed himself, Driver Simpson was found guilty of the murder of Fireman Dawson, and a deodand* of £2,000 was imposed on locomotives 15 and 82. The Directors of the London & Birmingham were reprimanded for employing Simpson.

The next accident of note happened thirty years later, on 26th. November, 1870. In its early years the North Western main line was still operated under the 'permissive' block system. This allowed two trains in the same section of line with a time interval between them. Signals were normally kept at 'all

* See page 84.

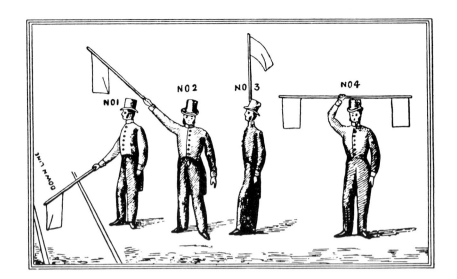

Instruction card issued to policemen on
the London & Birmingham Railway
before the introduction of fixed signals.
Courtesy Railway Gazette.

Attitude No. 1. — *Shews the RED
FLAG pointing to the Rails, to indicate
that the Train is to move slowly.*

Attitude No. 2. — *Pointed across the line
on which the Train is moving: if a
WHITE FLAG, shews that the line is
CLEAR, if a RED FLAG that the Train
is to STOP.*

Attitude No. 3. — *Brought to the
shoulder as the Train passes.*

Attitude No. 4. — *The united Flags held
by the middle of the staff in the right
hand above the head, across the line of
Railway, shews that assistance is wanted.*

clear' and were only placed at 'danger' for a period of ten minutes after the
passage of a train. The arrangements for fog signalling were also very vague.
During fog or falling snow a fog signalman should be stationed at distant
signals to relay the position of the signal arm to drivers by means of a
handlamp and detonators. The instructions for fogging duties were,
however, not well defined in the old rule books. The combination of the
permissive block, a thick fog, and a broken wagon coupling, were to spell
disaster at Harrow on that Saturday evening.

Just before 5.00 p.m. a heavy coal train left Willesden Junction on its run
to Harrow. This train was allowed only sixteen minutes to complete the five
and a half miles to Harrow *and* shunt clear of the main line, for close on its
heels was the 5 o'clock express from Euston to Liverpool and Manchester. As
the coal train was moved forward to shunt into Harrow yard, a wagon
coupling snapped, leaving half the train stranded on the Down line. It was
not until the Foreman at Harrow had heard the break-away that the fog
signalmen were ordered out, but by then it was too late.

The signalman at Harrow telegraphed Wembley Cutting Box, and the
signal there was placed at danger, but the double-headed express ran through
at full speed. Harrow Down Distant and Home signals were at caution and
danger respectively; and the coal train crew were trying desperately to reunite
the parted train with a spare coupling. Porter White ran back along the
Down line waving a red handlamp and placing detonators on the rails, but
he had only managed to cover 300 yards before the express came speeding
through the fog. The coal train had just been coupled back together when,
128 yards north of the Down Home signal, the express ploughed into the
back of it with catastrophic results. There were seven deaths, including
Driver Shelvey on the leading engine who was criticized for driving too fast
in the fog. Forty others were injured. G. P. Neele, Superintendent of the Line,
went down to Harrow by special train later that evening. "The wrecked train,
the blazing fitful light by which the men worked amid the 'debris' and the
dead, forms a ghastly reminiscence", he later wrote. Both Up and Down lines
were blocked until 2 o'clock the following morning.

An interesting account of this accident appeared in *The New Penny
Magazine* some 29 years later. The story was related to the anonymous writer
by a Station Master at a West Country station. Driver Shelvey, whose
nickname was 'Duke' because of his big Wellingtonian nose, was well known
on the North Western. He had rescued a stray dog from some porters at
Euston who were teasing the animal, and he christened it 'Snatch'. The dog
became Driver Shelvey's faithful companion and always travelled on the
locomotive with him. It was said that Snatch could even read the signals.

On that fateful evening of 26th. November, 1870, their Liverpool/
Manchester train had an uneventful run from Euston through Willesden
Junction (there is no mention of the fog in this account), and Driver Shelvey
and his fireman then decided to have their 'grub'. Snatch was called down
from his post on the front of the tender and given a bone to pick on the

footplate. It was while they were eating that the train ran through the signals at Wembley and Harrow. Snatch stayed on the engine and was uninjured, but pined for his dead master. The fireman was "...hurled over the Harrow Station, and fell into an empty truck in an adjoining siding, terribly mangled".

Snatch was immortalized in a wood engraving by animal artist Mr. Harrison Weir. The engraving was hanging in the Station Master's office at the unidentified West Country station where this story was told. It would be interesting to know if it still exists.

The third accident, or rather disaster, occurred on 8th. October, 1952, and again involved a train running through danger signals. Fog was also to play its part once more. Three trains were involved, their details being as follows:

(1)   The 7.31 a.m. Up Tring-Euston local train, hauled by 2-6-4 tank engine No.42389 running bunker first. This train normally consisted of seven 3rd. class coaches, but because of signalling and track alterations at Euston the following local train was cancelled, so two extra coaches were added to the 7.31 making nine in all.

(2)   The 8.15 p.m. (previous evening) Up Perth-Euston express, hauled by 4-6-2 'Princess Coronation' class locomotive No.46242 *City of Glasgow*. This train consisted of 11 bogie vehicles, including four sleeping cars and three vans.

(3)   The 8.00 a.m. Down Euston-Liverpool/Manchester express, double headed by 4-6-0 'Jubilee' class locomotive No.45637 *Windward Isles* (pilot engine) and 4-6-2 'Princess Royal' class locomotive No.46202 *Princess Anne* (train engine). 46202 was originally an experimental steam turbine locomotive, but had recently been converted to normal 4-cylinder propulsion. The train consisted of 15 bogie vehicles, including four vans at the rear.

Signalman A. G. Armitage came on duty at Harrow No.1 Box at 6.00 a.m. on Wednesday, 8th. October. It was foggy, but he could still see his 'fog object' which was the back lights of the Up Slow Home signals, 303 yards from the signal box. The regulations stipulated that the fog object should be 200 yards away, but this was interpreted liberally, and the error here was definitely on the safety side. By 6.35 a.m., a little over half an hour before sunrise, the fog had become thicker and Armitage could no longer see his fog object. The Harrow No.1 Distant signals were colour lights which penetrated

"Snatch" with Driver Shelvey on the footplate of their locomotive, as pictured in The New Penny Magazine. *Courtesy Dilwyn Chambers.*

The Grand Priory of
The Order of the Hospital of St. John of Jerusalem in England.
AMBULANCE DEPARTMENT.
The St. John Ambulance Association.

Patron :
HIS MOST GRACIOUS MAJESTY KING GEORGE V.
(Sovereign Head and Patron of the Order).

President:
FIELD-MARSHAL HIS ROYAL HIGHNESS THE DUKE OF CONNAUGHT. K.G.
(Grand Prior of the Order).

Director of the Ambulance Department and Chairman of Committee :
THE RIGHT HONOURABLE THE EARL OF PLYMOUTH. P.C.. C.B.

Assistant Director and Deputy Chairman :	Deputy Chairman :	Chief Secretary :
LIEUT-COLONEL SIR RICHARD C. TEMPLE. Br., C.I.E.	SIR JOHN FURLEY. C.B.	COLONEL SIR HERBERT C. PERROTT. Br., C.B
Director of Stores and Accountant :	Storekeeper :	Assistant Secretary :
WILLIAM R. EDWARDS. ESQ., A.C.A.	W. H. MORGAN, ESQ.	DUNCAN G. MONTEITH, ESQ.

This is to certify that *Charles D. J. Cawley* has attended a course of Instruction under the **London and North Western Railway** Centre of the St. John Ambulance Association, at *Harrow* and is qualified to render "First Aid to the Injured."

President of Centre.

Surgeon Instructor.

Surgeon Examiner

ST. JOHN'S GATE, CLERKENWELL,

LONDON, E.C. *March,* 1914.

Centre Secretary.

An LNWR First Aid Certificate issued at Harrow.

Courtesy Charles F. Cawley.

the fog, and therefore did not require fog signalmen stationed at them. All the other signals on the main lines were semaphores, and fog signalmen were required at the Outer Homes. However, no fog signalmen were available, so Armitage commenced 'fog block' working. This meant that an Up Fast train could not be accepted into his section unless it had a clear run through Harrow & Wealdstone Station for at least a quarter of a mile beyond the Inner Home signal.

We now join Signalman Armitage in Harrow No.1 Box a little after 8 a.m. to follow the unfortunate sequence of events:

8.07   The 7.31 a.m. Tring-Euston local train is accepted from Hatch End Box on the Up Slow line.

8.10   The fog object is now visible and Signalman Armitage reverts to normal block working. This means that a train can be accepted from Hatch End on the Up Fast line with the Harrow No.1 Distant at caution, and the Outer Home and Inner Home signals at danger protecting a train already in Harrow & Wealdstone Station.

8.11   The 8.15 p.m. (previous evening) Perth-Euston express is accepted from Hatch End Box on the Up Fast line. The Up Fast signals are maintained at danger.

8.14   The 'Train Entering Section' bell is received for the Tring-Euston local. This train approaches Harrow & Wealdstone on the Up Slow line and crosses over onto the Up Fast line at Harrow No.1 Box in accordance with the working timetable. Residential services were, in any event, given precedence over any late running overnight expresses from the North. The local train was to run non-stop to Euston after its halt at Harrow & Wealdstone.

8.17   The Tring-Euston local arrives at Platform 4 (Up Fast). It is running seven minutes late due to fog on the journey from Tring.

-do.-   The Perth-Euston express passes Hatch End on the Up Fast running approximately 80 minutes late, again due to fog which had been particularly bad between Crewe and Rugby.

-do.- The 'Train Entering Section' bell is received for the Perth-Euston express. The Up Fast signals are still at danger protecting the local train in Platform 4.

-do.- The 'Train Entering Section' bell is received from North Wembley Box for the 8.00 a.m. Euston-Liverpool/Manchester express on the Down Fast line. This train had left Euston five minutes late due to a minor vacuum defect, but being double-headed it is regaining lost time. With the Down Fast signals clear it is travelling at about 60 m.p.h.

8.18 Signalman Armitage is astonished to hear the sound of the Perth-Euston express approaching at speed, and he sees it coming out of the mist and passsing his Up Fast Outer Home at danger (a distance of nearly 600 yards from the signal box). It is travelling at about 55 m.p.h. and making no attempt to stop.

-do.- The Tring-Euston local in Platform 4 is packed with 800 or so passengers; many are standing. Guard W. H. Merritt had given permission for some passengers to stand in his brake compartment in the 7th. coach. He then walked back to the 8th. and 9th. (last) coaches to shut some of the doors. As he is doing so he at first hears, and then sees, the Perth-Euston express approaching at speed behind his train. Guard Merritt shouts a warning and then runs for his life across the platform and jumps onto the Down Slow line.

-do.- Signalman Armitage places detonators on the Up Fast line from a lever in his box, and the Perth-Euston express makes a full brake application at the last second, but it is too late. Armitage also throws his Down Fast signals to danger, but just as he does so the annunciator buzzer for track circuit No.2776 sounds in his box, indicating that the Euston-Liverpool/Manchester express is already at the Down Fast Outer Home, just 200 yards from the road bridge at the south end of the station. The footplate crews on the Liverpool/Manchester engines do not see the signal return to danger.

8.18½ The inevitable happens. The Perth-Euston express ploughs into the local train at Platform 4. The locomotive comes to rest on the adjacent Down Fast line under the station footbridge. The shock wave from the collision stops all the station clocks. (The tower clock stopped at 8.19½, but this was always kept one minute fast.) A second or so later the Liverpool/Manchester express bursts upon the scene and hits the locomotive of the Perth-Euston train. The engines of the double-headed Liverpool/Manchester express mount Platform 3, cross Platform 2 which islands it, and finish on their sides on the Up D.C. electric New Line, thereby cutting off the current which stops an approaching Up train well clear of the obstruction. The signalman at Harrow No. 2 Box, which controls only the New Line, turns off the current to the Down electric line.

-do.- Signalman Armitage at Harrow No.1 Box, having witnessed not one disaster but two, retains his senses and sends the 6-beat 'Obstruction-Danger' bell for all lines to Hatch End and North Wembley boxes, and records the fact in his train register.

8.19 Guard Merritt emerges from under the coping of Platform 5 on the Down Slow line. The last three coaches of his Tring-Euston local have disappeared.

-do.- Guard J. Kent of the Perth-Euston express climbs down from his van at the undamaged rear of his train. Both guards go to the signal box and are assured by Armitage that all lines are protected by danger signals. Guards Merritt and Kent are surprised to find later that the Liverpool/Manchester express had already run into the wreckage of their own trains.

8.22 The first ambulance and doctor arrive, with the Police and Fire

Brigade close behind. Rescue work commences on the pile of 13 coaches in the centre of the station which had been compressed into a heap of wreckage 45 yards long, 18 yards wide, and 30 feet high. Part of the station footbridge was broken.

8.28   Station Master C. S. Rolinson makes his way to Harrow No.1 Box and finds Signalman Armitage "deathly white" and very upset. He is helped out of the box and sits on the steps to get some air. The Station Master returns to the rescue work...

Valuable assistance with the rescue operations was provided by a medical unit of the United States Air Force, the Women's Royal Voluntary Service, the Salvation Army (who provided a canteen), priests and ministers of several denominations, local residents, and engineering firms who lent staff and equipment. Railway staff along the line were also released from their normal duties in order to help with the rescue work. A casualty clearing station was set-up across the tracks at the north end of Platform 7 (stranding the Belmont Branch train in the station), and casualties were then transferred to waiting ambulances in the goods yard. A control office was established in the Belmont Branch waiting room.

Breakdown cranes arrived from Willesden, Rugby, Kentish Town, Crewe, and Old Oak Common. Although the Up and Down Slow lines had been undamaged in the accident, it was necessary to close all lines as they were required for the breakdown cranes, and a clear path across the tracks had to be kept for the evacuation of casualties. It was not until 1.30 a.m. on the following morning, the 9th. October, that there appeared to be no chance at all of anyone still being found alive in the debris. 102 persons had lost their lives, and a further 10 died later in hospital. In addition, 157 injured were taken to local hospitals, and another 183 were treated at the station for minor injury or shock. This death roll has only once been exceeded in an accident on the railways of Great Britain — the double collision at Quintinshill, Gretna, on 22nd. May, 1915, in which 227 persons were killed.

With the closure of all lines through Harrow & Wealdstone the dislocation of traffic was widespread, with most Euston services being dealt with at Saint Pancras or Paddington. On the New Line, Up trains were terminated at Hatch End and Down trains at Wembley Central, with London Transport providing a special bus service in between. The Slow lines were re-opened to traffic early on 9th. October, but with breakdown cranes still working on the New and Fast lines they were not re-opened until early on 11th. October and the evening of 12th. October respectively. A temporary station footbridge was available by the evening of 12th. October, and a new permanent span across the Fast lines was brought into use on 9th. November.

At the ensuing Ministry of Transport Inquiry the Chief Inspecting Officer of Railways, Lieutenant Colonel G. R. S. Wilson, was satisfied that no responsibility for the accident should rest with Signalman Armitage. Driver R. S. Jones and Fireman C. Turnock of the Perth-Euston express both lost their lives in the accident, and we shall never know why they ran through the signals at danger. The Inspector urged the adoption of an automatic warning system which would give an audible and visual warning in the locomotive cab when signals were passed at caution or danger, with a subsequent brake application. Experiments with the later adopted inductive system were already in hand when the Harrow & Wealdstone disaster struck.

The driver on the leading engine of the Liverpool/Manchester express also lost his life, but the fireman, G. Cowper, had a remarkable escape. Like the fireman in the 1870 accident, he was thrown from the locomotive cab, but instead of landing in a coal truck he found himself lying on the upturned wheel splasher of the second engine.

It is said that things happen in threes; let's hope that is true and Harrow & Wealdstone will not see any more accidents with such terrible loss of life. Significant anniversaries of the 1952 disaster are still remembered in the local newspaper, and for many years a wreath was placed on one of the station flower beds on 8th. October.

ACCIDENTS WILL HAPPEN . . .

The Harrow & Wealdstone disaster, 8th.
October, 1952, looking north from the
footbridge. Breakdown cranes tackle the
pile of wreckage from the three trains
while rescuers still search for survivors.
In the background, from left to right,
can be seen a breakdown train on the
Down New Line, a Bakerloo Line train
in Electrified Siding No. 1, and Harrow
No. 1 Box, where Signalman A.G.
Armitage watched helplessly as disaster
followed disaster. In the foreground can
be seen the edge of Platform 5, where
Guard W.H. Merritt crouched under the
coping while the rear of his Tring-Euston
local train was destroyed.
            Central Press Photos Ltd.

95

The view from Platform 1, looking north, on 8th. October, 1952. The Liverpool/Manchester express is sprawled across platforms 2 and 3.

Central Press Photos Ltd.

The pilot engine of the Liverpool/Manchester express, ex-LMS 'Jubilee' class 4-6-0 No. 45637 Windward Isles, *after it had been re-railed on the New Line Electrified Siding No. 2 on 9th. October. The remains of the locomotive were cut up.*

Central Press Photos Ltd.

The train engine of the Liverpool/Manchester express, ex-LMS 'Princess Royal' class 4-6-2 No. 46202 Princess Anne, is lifted from its resting position on the Up New Line on 9th. October. This locomotive was also scrapped, but the engine of the Perth-Euston express (buried under the footbridge) was less severely damaged and was returned to service.

Central Press Photos Ltd.

ACCIDENT AT HARROW AND W

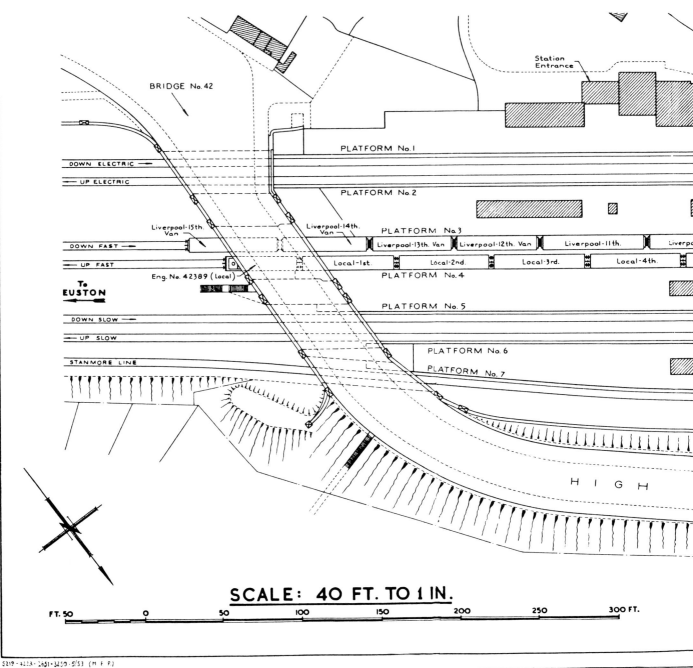

BRIDGE No. 42

Station
Entrance

PLATFORM No. 1

DOWN ELECTRIC

UP ELECTRIC

PLATFORM No. 2

Liverpool-15th.
Van

Liverpool-14th.
Van

PLATFORM No. 3

Liverpool-13th. Van   Liverpool-12th. Van   Liverpool-11th.   Liverpo

DOWN FAST

UP FAST

Local-1st.   Local-2nd.   Local-3rd.   Local-4th.

Eng. No. 42389 (Local)

PLATFORM No. 4

To EUSTON

PLATFORM No. 5

DOWN SLOW

UP SLOW

PLATFORM No. 6

STANMORE LINE

PLATFORM No. 7

H I G H

SCALE: 40 FT. TO 1 IN.

FT. 50   0   50   100   150   200   250   300 FT.

S219 · 4223 · 2651 · 3250 · 5/53 (M F P.)

RESULTS OF THE TWO COLLISIONS

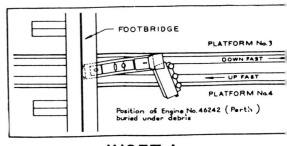

FOOTBRIDGE

PLATFORM No. 3

DOWN FAST

UP FAST

PLATFORM No. 4

Position of Engine No. 46242 (Perth)
buried under debris

INSET A

Part of the plan shewing the results of the two collisions at Harrow & Wealdstone on 8th. October, 1952, from the Ministry of Transport's official accident report. The plan is reproduced here at a reduced scale.

Reproduced with the permission of the Controller of Her Majesty's Stationery Office. Crown Copyright Reserved.

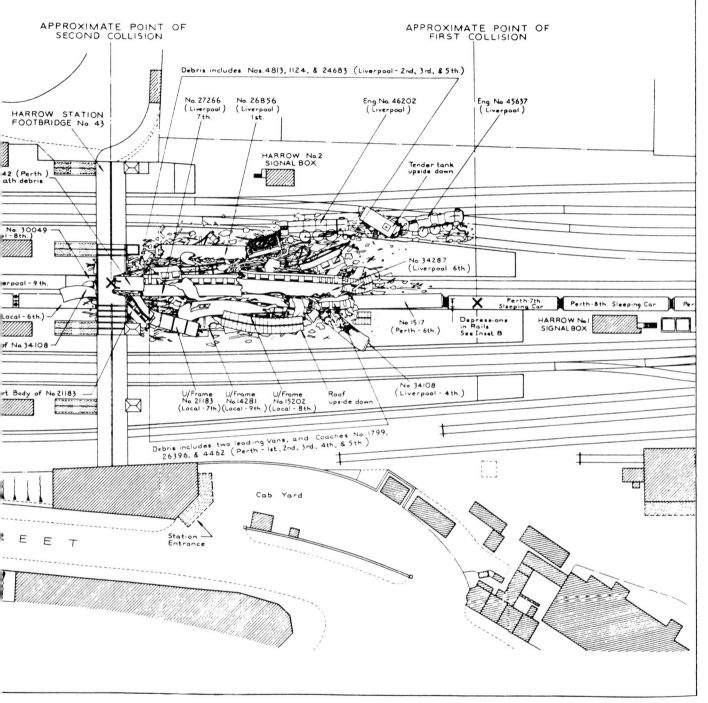

APPROXIMATE POINT OF
SECOND COLLISION

APPROXIMATE POINT OF
FIRST COLLISION

Debris includes Nos. 4813, 1124, & 24683 (Liverpool - 2nd, 3rd, & 5th.)

HARROW STATION
FOOTBRIDGE No. 43

No. 27266
(Liverpool)
7th.

No. 26856
(Liverpool)
1st.

Eng. No. 46202
(Liverpool)

Eng. No. 45637
(Liverpool)

HARROW No. 2
SIGNAL BOX

Tender tank
upside down

42 (Perth)
ath debris

No. 30049
l - 8th.)

No. 34287
(Liverpool 6th.)

erpool - 9 th.

Perth-7th.
Sleeping Car

Perth-8th. Sleeping Car

Per

Local - 6th.)

No. 1517
(Perth - 6th.)

Depressions
in Rails
See Inset B

HARROW No. 1
SIGNAL BOX

of No. 34108

t Body of No. 21183

U/Frame
No. 21183
(Local - 7th.)

U/Frame
No. 14281
(Local - 9th.)

U/Frame
No. 15202
(Local - 8th.)

Roof
upside down

No. 34108
(Liverpool - 4th.)

Debris includes two leading Vans, and Coaches No. 1799,
26396, & 4462 (Perth - 1st, 2nd, 3rd, 4th, & 5th.)

Cab Yard

R E E T

Station
Entrance

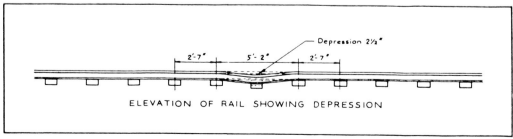

Depression 2½"

2'-7"   5'-2"   2'-7"

ELEVATION OF RAIL SHOWING DEPRESSION

INSET B

The overhead wires are up, and work is progressing on the reconstruction of the A409 road bridge at Harrow & Wealdstone. This view was taken at the beginning of October, 1964, during the final week of operation of the Belmont Branch train which is passing under the bridge.

Geoffrey Kichenside.

A 'mechanical horse' and trailer stand outside Harrow & Wealdstone Station on 30th. April, 1966, before touring the area to advertise Harrow Rail Week. Part of the exhibition train can be seen in the Belmont Branch platform on the right.

Peter G. Scott.

9 'HARROW RAIL WEEK', 1966

"A big change is taking place in the way trains are hauled. Steam engines are being replaced by diesel and electric engines. Many miles of lines, including main lines, are being electrified. Thousands of electric and diesel engines and trains are to be used".

From *All Along the Line* (British Transport Commission, 1959).

'Harrow Rail Week' was held in May, 1966, as a celebration to promote the new a.c. electric main line services between Euston, Liverpool and Manchester. For the beginning of this story, however, we must go back to 1954. It was in December of that year that the British Transport Commission published their £1,500 million plan for the Modernization and Re-equipment of British Railways (usually referred to as the '*1955* Modernization Plan'). Steam locomotives, although still being built, were to be replaced by diesel and electric traction.

The subsequent hasty transition from steam to diesel resulted in almost new BR 'Standard' type steam locomotives, still with a good 40 years working life in them, being sent to the scrap yards to be replaced by a varied collection of unproven diesel types.* Many of these early diesels have already gone for scrap. In hindsight, the money invested in diesel traction might have been better expended in electrifying the railways while the steam fleet worked out its useful life. There was, however, an important electrification scheme carried out as a direct result of the 1955 Modernization Plan. This was the London Midland Region Euston to Liverpool and Manchester scheme on which survey work commenced in 1957. The cost of the electrification, as estimated in 1959, was £175 million.

It was originally intended to electrify the line at 1.5kV direct current with overhead wires. A new overhead system, however, had been developed in France, and this gave certain advantages over the 1.5kV D.C. system which had been the standard in this country. The new system used 25kV single phase alternating current on the standard industrial frequency of 50 cycles per second. It was this method that was adopted for the Euston Main Line and for all subsequent overhead electrifications in Great Britain.

In addition to equipping for electrification, the London Midland scheme included new track layouts, new signalling and telecommunications, and the complete rebuilding of some stations. It involved the construction of a new railway on top of the old, but carried out whilst keeping the lines in virtually full operation. The old Euston Station was swept away, and the battle to save the Euston Arch† — the 'trade mark' of the West Coast Route and monument to the railway age — was lost.

The work of erecting the overhead wires and their supporting masts was mechanized to a high degree. A large auger borer was used for making holes in the ground for the steel masts; wiring trains carrying drums of wire followed the masts and as the wire was run out the necessary connexions were made. A total of 300 overline bridges required alteration because there was insufficient clearance for the overhead wires. The bridge at the south end of Harrow & Wealdstone Station, carrying the A409 road, had to be completely rebuilt.

To make the line safe for 100 m.p.h. running it was resignalled with colour-lights and the Automatic Warning System provided throughout. A total of 212 mechanical signal boxes were abolished; Harrow No.1 and Hatch End boxes were closed in 1964. The line from Euston to north of Rugby is now

* The fact that there is still a large number of steam locomotives working in Great Britain today is due to the wisdom of just one scrap merchant, Dai Woodham of Barry, South Wales. He purchased over 200 steam engines from BR but never cut them up. Most of them have since been sold to preservation societies and privately operated railways.

† In fact it was neither an arch nor a portico, but a propylaeum.

controlled by only five power signal boxes, situated at Euston, Willesden, Watford, Bletchley, and Rugby. The Watford installation controls the 28 mile section of main line from North Wembley to Cheddington, and this area includes four self-contained satellité relay interlockings at Harrow & Wealdstone, King's Langley, Hemel Hempstead, and Tring.

From September, 1965, some freight trains passing through Harrow were electrically hauled, and in November electric traction appeared on some passenger workings. Various overnight services which had been diverted to Marylebone during the Euston rebuilding were returned to Euston, and by 3rd. January, 1966, all passenger trains on the Euston Main Line were electrically hauled. The revised and accelerated timetable came into operation on 18th. April, 1966. Just two weeks later, it was Harrow & Wealdstone's turn to play host to the 'Britain's New Railway' exhibition train which was the main feature of Harrow Rail Week.

The exhibition train, together with one of the new blue and white liveried 3,300 h.p. electric locomotives, was parked in Harrow & Wealdstone's Platform 7 which latterly served the Belmont Branch. The Rail Week, from Monday, 2nd. May to Saturday, 7th. May, also included competitions, a balloon race, cheap trips, and an exhibition and films at the Granada Cinema. The cheap trips were by special trains to Coventry (twice daily except Monday) for 10/- and Chester (Saturday only) for 19/-. The Chester train was a locomotive hauled Inter-City express, but the Coventry trips were worked by the new electric multiple units used on the outer suburban services.

The 25kV overhead electrification was later extended all the way to Glasgow over the West Coast Route. The full Euston — Glasgow electric service, dubbed '*The Electric Scots*', was inaugurated on 6th. May, 1974, with a journey time of five hours on the fastest train. In the meantime, work had been progressing on the high-speed Advanced Passenger Train (A.P.T.) which would cut the journey time even further. It was planned to have a full service of A.P.T.'s on the West Coast Route by the early 1980's.

Unfortunately, the Advanced Passenger Train was a promise unfulfilled. A great deal of experience and knowledge was gained from the project, but the A.P.T. itself never achieved its overall objectives. The train featured a tilt mechanism to enable it to negotiate curves at high speed, but this mechanism often caused problems when running. One of the prototype trains, however, did reach 162 m.p.h., and a test run from Euston to Glasgow on 12th. December, 1984, was completed in the record time of 3 hours 52 minutes 40 seconds. This train ran through Harrow & Wealdstone at 127 m.p.h., and through Hatch End at 127½ m.p.h.

With the recent resurrection of the Channel Tunnel project we may even eventually see a version of the French High-Speed Train — the *Train à Grande Vitesse* — running through Harrow. But that, if it ever happens, would not be before 1993 at the earliest. George Findlay (see page 13) would be rather surprised.

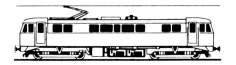

Opposite page: *An extract from the programme for Harrow Rail Week, and a souvenir ticket for one of the Coventry trips.*
Peter G. Scott's collection, reproduced courtesy British Rail,
London Midland Region.

 **British Rail**

ADMISSION
FREE

BRITAIN'S NEW RAILWAY
EXHIBITION

HARROW AND WEALDSTONE STATION   MAY 2nd — 7th 10.00 — 21.00 hours

The fascinating story of the building of Britain's NEW Railway

★ Automatic Train Control
★ Colour-light Signalling
★ Train describer
★ Long-welded-rail Exhibit, and many other features
★ See the story in film in the cinema
★ Don't forget the balloon race — 6d

FREE TRAVEL FROM LOCAL STATIONS TO THE EXHIBITION

GRANADA HARROW
HAR 1946

BRITISH RAIL EXHIBITION
and
display of winning entries in painting and photographic
competitions

SATURDAY, MAY 7th
at 11.00 hours
Specially Compiled Programme
**BRITAIN'S NEW
RAILWAY**
The whole fascinating story in colour
—
*Invitations free from British Rail
Agents and Stations*

**MOBILE ENQUIRY
BUREAU**
—
All information about Britain's
New Railway
—
TIMES – FARES – FACILITIES
—
OUTSIDE THE GRANADA

British Rail | London Midland Region | N⁰ 227

SOUVENIR TICKET
VALID ONLY FOR
HARROW RAIL WEEK SPECIAL TRAIN
HARROW & WEALDSTONE
to COVENTRY AND BACK

7th MAY 1966

TO MARK COMPLETION OF MAIN LINE ELECTRIFICATION
LONDON - LIVERPOOL - MANCHESTER

Fare 10/0

This ticket may be retained.   For Conditions – See over.

British Rail 25kV a.c. electric locomotive No. E3149 at the head of the Harrow Rail Week exhibition train in Platform 7 at Harrow & Wealdstone. The locomotive obviously did not work into the platform under its own power as no part of the branch to Belmont and Stanmore Village was ever electrified. This view (with the goods shed in the background) and the picture below were taken on 30th. April, 1966, before the exhibition opened.

Peter G. Scott.

Main line electric to Stanmore Village! A head-on view of E3149 displaying a 'special' headcode. This locomotive was renumbered 86 246 in 1974, and was named Royal Anglian Regiment at a ceremony at Liverpool Street on 13th. May, 1985. It had originally been intended to use the name Scafell Pike for 86 246.

Peter G. Scott.

*One of the special Harrow Rail Week excursions to Coventry departs from
Platform 5 at Harrow & Wealdstone on 7th. May, 1966.*

Peter G. Scott.

The Harrow Rail Week exhibition train in Platform 7.   Peter G. Scott.

*The Advanced Passenger Train, now unfortunately scrapped. New streamlined
electric locomotives are, however, due to appear on the West Coast Route
during 1987/8.*

Central Photographic Unit, British Railways Board.

10 ALONG THE LINE . . .

Everyday views along the line from Kenton to Hatch End, and on the Stanmore Village Branch. The illustrations are generally arranged topographically from south to north.

Part 1 KENTON

Kenton is a New Line station, opened to passengers on 15th. June, 1912, although it also had a goods yard, opened on 13th. March, 1911, connected to the main lines. The station acquired the suffix 'for Northwick Park' which was later gradually dropped, but did not disappear from timetables until comparatively recent years. The goods yard was closed on and from 3rd. May, 1965, and is currently used as a rubbish tip; a plan for a large supermarket was recently refused planning permission. The station is just outside the boundary of the present London Borough of Harrow, but is included here as 50 per cent of its catchment area is within the borough.

LNWR 'Claughton' class 4-6-0 No. 162 heads a fine assortment of carriages on a Down Liverpool express near Kenton in about 1922. This view was taken from the footbridge on the Sheepcote Lane — Woodcock Dell path (this bridge now connects Northwick Park to Conway Gardens).
London & North Western Railway Society collection.

From the same footbridge, but looking in the opposite direction, ex-LNWR
'Claughton' class 4-6-0 No. 1092 hauls an Up Manchester — Euston express in
1923. In the background can be seen a Metropolitan Railway train and the roof of
the LNWR New Line electricity sub-station.

London & North Western Railway Society collection.

The 'Locomotive Exchanges' of 1948. After nationalization, locomotives of the
former 'Big Four' companies were tried out on each others' lines so that a
standard design could be evaluated for future BR motive power. Here ex-
Southern Railway 'Merchant Navy' class 4-6-2 No. 35017 Belgian Marine *heads*
an Up train under the Metropolitan and Great Central lines at Kenton. The first
carriage is a Dynamometer Car for recording the locomotive's performance.

Locomotive Publishing Company, courtesy Ian Allan.

LNWR 'Precedent' class 2-4-0 No. 955 Charles Dickens *on a Down express passes under the distinctive footbridge that carried the Sheepcote Lane — Woodcock Hill footpath across the tracks. This view was taken in 1900, and some ten years later the footbridge was rebuilt when the New Line was put through, and it now connects Northwick Avenue with The Ridgeway. In the background can be seen the Metropolitan Railway bridge.*

Locomotive & General Railway Photographs, courtesy David & Charles.

An unidentified 'Precedent' heads an Up Carlisle — Euston train under the same footbridge on 29th. August, 1906. The second carriage is a 12-wheeled dining saloon.

London & North Western Railway Society collection.

*An Up semi-fast train from Northampton, unusually hauled by an ex-LMS
'Princess Royal' 4-6-2, passes Kenton Goods Yard on the Up Fast line in about
1959. The adjacent Down Slow line has just been relaid, replacing the former
short-length rails which had been put in during the Second World War. The
change in wheel beat was usually enough to rouse Wealdstone bound commuters
from their slumbers in time for the stop at Harrow & Wealdstone.*

Geoffrey Kichenside.

Ex-LMS 'Princess Royal' class 4-6-2 No. 46211 Queen Maud *passes the 10¼ mile
post at Kenton in May, 1958, with the Down* Royal Highlander *bound for
Inverness. Coal wagons can be seen in the goods yard on the extreme left, and in
the background is the girder footbridge that replaced the wooden structure
pictured on the opposite page.*

C.R.L. Coles.

Station Master D.G. Evans stands beside the station garden at Kenton in 1960. Also pictured in this view is the old signal box, and the once familiar gas lamp columns.

Donald G. Evans.

Kenton Station and garden in 1963. A train of BR Standard stock departs on the Up New Line.

Courtesy Donald G. Evans.

ALONG THE LINE . . .

The garden on the Down-side cutting at Kenton was a delight to behold, and it won many first prizes in the station gardens competition. The December, 1961, issue of the *British Railways London Midland Magazine* reported:

> "Passengers on the Euston electric lines have not been slow to show to Stationmaster D.G. Evans their appreciation of the garden at Kenton. 'As a regular traveller from your station, I should like to congratulate you and your staff upon the beautiful station garden', writes the chairman of Kenton Horticultural Society.... 'Your station is a thing of beauty and a joy to see in passing through to London', says a season-ticket holder from Bushey...."

Station gardens have long been a railway tradition. As early as 22nd. February, 1843, the London & Birmingham's Coaching and Police Committee ordered that "Two rakes and hoes to be supplied to stations for the use of Porters during intervals between trains".

Pictured below, and on the opposite page (lower), is part of the award-winning display mounted to celebrate the centenary of the International Red Cross in 1963. Sadly, this magnificent garden is no more, and the area has returned to nature.

Courtesy Donald G. Evans.

The exterior of Kenton for Northwick Park Station viewed in April, 1933 (above), and the widened Kenton Bridge as it appeared in January, 1928 (below). The present borough boundary between Harrow and Brent runs along the middle of the bridge. It is worth noting here that a number of the New Line stations were of similar design, Kenton and Headstone Lane (see page 132) being among them.

London Regional Transport.

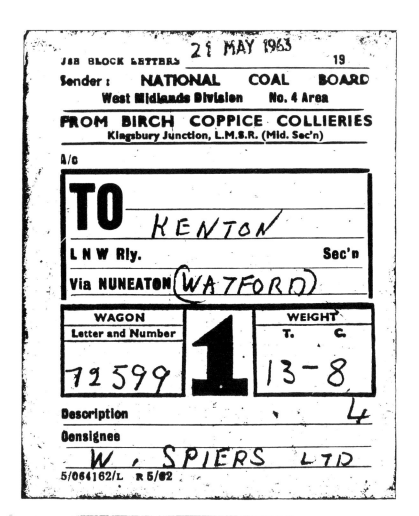

Wagon label from a consignment of coal to Kenton in 1963. Note that the old railway company names (LMS, Midland, and LNWR) are still in use Wallace Spiers' coal office was in Kenton Road by the goods yard entrance, and was notable in having an enormous lump of coal positioned outside. A large direction sign to the coal office can be seen outside the station entrance in the views on the opposite page.
Peter G. Scott's collection.

Ex-LNWR 'Prince of Wales' class 4-6-0s Nos. 5684 Arabic *and 5685* Persia *head the Euston — Cardington R101 airship Funeral Special through Kenton on 11th. October, 1930. This view was taken from the footbridge at the end of Bonnersfield Lane, Greenhill. The Kenton Bridge is in the background.*
Locomotive Publishing Company, courtesy Ian Allan.

LNWR 'G1' class 0-8-0 No. 93 hauls an Up coal train of nearly 70 trucks in this war-time (1914-18) view taken from the Bonnersfield Lane footbridge. These superheated 0-8-0 locomotives were also generally known as 'Super D's. Note that the conductor rails have just been laid on the Down New Line; those for the Up line are laying in the 'six-foot' between the tracks.

Locomotive Publishing Company, courtesy Ian Allan.

Another view from the Bonnersfield Lane footbridge. Ex-LMS Stanier 8F 2-8-0 No. 48762 hauls an Up mixed freight past the Kenton Recreation Ground on 6th. August, 1953.

British Rail, London Midland Region.

The three illustrations on this page all shew trains on the Down Slow line, taken from more or less the same viewpoint near Dirty Lane (Elmgrove Road). In the view above (taken from a commercial postcard) an unidentified LNWR 4-4-2 'Precursor Tank' heads a local train of six-wheelers. The track on the far right is the contractor's line in connexion with the New Line construction.

Courtesy Dilwyn Chambers.

An unidentified LNWR 0-6-2 'Coal Tank' on a special train of six-wheeled stock. The ground has been prepared for the New Line tracks on the right.

London & North Western Railway Society collection.

A double-headed goods train photographed in 1911. The leading locomotive is a 'G' class 0-8-0 No. 1401 (with a 'piano' front), and the train engine is a '19in. Goods' 4-6-0. The pair of tall signals — guyed together — with co-acting repeater arms at eye level, refer to the Down Slow and Down Fast lines (the Slow line arms are ringed). They will soon be repositioned as work progresses on the New Line; the Down track is already in place.

Locomotive Publishing Company, courtesy Ian Allan.

Part 2 HARROW & WEALDSTONE

As noted in Chapter 2, this station was originally called Harrow Weald, but its name was shortened to Harrow on or soon after its opening date of 20th. July, 1837. The station's present name was adopted on 1st. May, 1897, but it is known locally as Wealdstone because of its position. The goods yard was closed on and from 3rd. April, 1967.

LNWR 4-6-2 'Superheater Tank' No. 1366 heads an Up express away from Harrow & Wealdstone. The New Lines on the left are not yet in use as the rails are unpolished.

Locomotive Publishing Company, courtesy Ian Allan.

LNWR 'Jubilee' class 4-4-0 No. 1931 Agincourt *on a Down express approaching Harrow & Wealdstone in 1901. Beyond the Down Slow line signal can be seen the roof of the original Harrow No. 1 signal box. The Stanmore Branch trails away in the left background.*

Locomotive & General Railway Photographs, courtesy David & Charles.

An official LNWR postcard view of 'Greater Britain' class 2-2-2-2 Compound
No. 528 Richard Moon *with a Rugby express "passing Harrow". Sir Richard*
Moon was Chairman of the London & North Western Railway from 1861 to 1891.
London & North Western Railway Society collection.

Another view of 'Precedent' class 2-4-0 No. 955 Charles Dickens, *this time*
entering Harrow & Wealdstone Station with the 4.00 p.m. express from Euston on
31st. May, 1902. The train is on the Down Fast line, which later became the Down
New Line, and is about to pass under the additional footbridge provided at the
south end of the station after the Harrow & Stanmore Railway opened. Note that
the line to Stanmore is well advertised on the running-in board.
Locomotive Club of Great Britain, Ken Nunn collection.

LNWR 2-4-2 '5ft. 6in. Tank' No. 1184 waits under the south footbridge at Harrow & Wealdstone for the 'right away' on the Up Slow line. Above the stairs leading down to the platform there is a sign (barely discernible) pointing to the "STANMORE TRAINS" on the far side of the platform. This picture was also taken on 31st. May, 1902.

Locomotive Club of Great Britain, Ken Nunn collection.

The Belmont Branch 'Park Royal' diesel unit leaves Platform 7 at Harrow & Wealdstone on its return journey to pick up more morning commuters on their way to London. This view was taken on 29th. September, 1964, during the last week that this useful service was in operation.

Geoffrey Kichenside.

The view from the new clock tower at Harrow & Wealdstone Station in 1912. The goods shed is on the left, and the junction of Wealdstone High Street and Masons Avenue on the right.

Harrow Local History Collection, London Borough of Harrow.

A similar view from the clock tower, taken in October, 1986. The coal offices (centre left) were built by the LNWR and bear the date "1913". A. Wooster & Sons (Coal and Coke Merchants, Carmen and Contractors) stated on their 1920's billhead that they were the "Oldest Established in the District", and they are still selling coal and coke from the same offices. In the background (centre right) is the rebuilt Queen's Arms public house. On the right-hand side the shops have altered very little. The large domed skylight above the booking hall can be seen in the foreground.

Ian Brown.

An early morning scene on Platform 1 at Harrow & Wealdstone in 1946. A train of pre-1938 clerestory-roofed Bakerloo Line stock is bound for Watford Junction.
C.R.L. Coles.

Tranquillity and speed — a trolley-load of flowers and a 100 m.p.h. express — Harrow & Wealdstone platforms 2 and 3, October, 1986. The four columns formerly supported the old middle footbridge.

Ian Brown.

Ex-LNWR Oerlikon stock at Platform 1 in May, 1957.

C.R.L. Coles.

A Down Bletchley local train standing at Platform 5, Harrow & Wealdstone, circa 1936. The locomotives are an ex-LNWR 'George the Fifth' class 4-4-0, No. 25393 Loyalty, *and an LMS Stanier 2-6-4 Tank.*

C.R.L. Coles.

An unidentified LNWR 'Jubilee' class 4-4-0 heads an Up train through Harrow & Wealdstone at around the turn of the century. The first vehicle behind the locomotive tender is a horse-box.
London & North Western Railway Society collection.

Another 'Jubilee', No. 1932 Anson, *heads an Up express through Harrow on 31st. May, 1902. The original Harrow No. 2 signal box can be seen on the right, and in the distance on the left are the Kodak factory and David Allen printing works.*
Locomotive Club of Great Britain, Ken Nunn collection.

LNWR 'E' class four-cylinder compound 2-8-0 No. 2558 stands on the Up Fast line at Harrow & Wealdstone in 1911. This freight locomotive originally started life as a 'B' class 0-8-0. The LNWR often used Staffordshire blue bricks with a lozenge pattern for platform surfaces, and examples can be seen in this picture. A few of these bricks can still be found at the north end of Platform 7.

Courtesy Hertfordshire Library Service, Watford Libraries.

Ex-LMS 'Princess Coronation' class 4-6-2 No. 46256 Sir William A. Stanier, F.R.S. *is relegated to freight duties, and is seen here passing Harrow No. 1 Box on the Up Fast line in 1962. The crossovers between the Slow and Fast lines have been moved from the north end of the station to the south end (hence only one arm on the Down Fast Inner Home signal), and a reverse crossover inserted further to the north. If the crossovers had been in these positions ten years earlier, the 1952 disaster would not have taken place.*

Geoffrey Kichenside.

Two views inside the original Harrow No. 2 signal box which controlled the main lines and sidings to the north of the station.

Above: *Signalling a train through in 1907.*

Real Photographs Company, courtesy Ian Allan.

Right: *An official LNWR postcard entitled "Accepting a train at Harrow". The signalman in this view is the same one that is performing the acrobatics in the background of the top picture.*

Courtesy Dilwyn Chambers.

The present Harrow No. 2 signal box, which was originally called Harrow New Line, pictured in October, 1986. The box is worked when trains are reversing in the New Line Electrified Sidings. When the re-signalling scheme is completed this box will become redundant.
Ian Brown.

Although controlling colour light signals, Harrow No. 2 still has a traditional mechanical lever frame with 18 levers (1 spare).
Ian Brown.

Cleaning the spectacle glasses of the Down Fast Inner Home signal at Harrow & Wealdstone. The right-hand arm is for the crossover to the Down Slow line, but from 1962 became the main Home arm when the crossover was moved to the south of the station (this arm was easier to sight).

C.R.L. Coles.

The lamp trimmer attends to an LNWR pattern miniature ground signal on the Up Slow line at Harrow & Wealdstone. The goods shed and the empty stock of the Belmont Branch train are in the background.

C.R.L. Coles.

The crane at Harrow & Wealdstone Goods Yard, pictured on 12th. March, 1958.
  British Rail, London Midland Region.

Below: *Headstone Drive railway bridge in January, 1953, looking towards Wealdstone High Street. The bus is a London Transport A.E.C. Regent Low Height vehicle, No. RLH 67, running on route 230 from Northwick Park Station to Rayner's Lane Station. During heavy rainfall the road under the bridge often floods. Similar flooding also used to occur at Christchurch Avenue Bridge on the Stanmore Village Branch.*
  London Regional Transport.

The LMS float for the annual Harrow Hospital Carnival, pictured in the early 1930's. On the left in each view is Driver Bob Bavin from the Goods Department at Harrow & Wealdstone, and on the right, holding publicity leaflets, is the Station Foreman, Charles D. Cawley. The trusty steed is from the railway stables that were situated in the goods yard, and the wagon load of mischief with their buckets and spades are the children of railway staff. The float is advertising "LMS SUMMER TICKETS — ANY TRAIN — ANY DAY". One of the most popular excursions was the 1/9d. return half-day Saturday afternoon trip to Southend-on-Sea, returning in the small hours of Sunday morning. This special train was often already full after leaving Watford, so a relief train would be started from the sidings at Harrow & Wealdstone.

Courtesy Charles F. Cawley.

A publicity photograph taken for the LMS shewing a C.O.D. delivery at Cecil Road, Wealdstone. Motor Driver Ted Croft delivers a new lawn mower to Dorothy Cawley. Four or five delivery vans operated from Harrow & Wealdstone, covering the area from Roxeth to Bushey Heath.

Courtesy Charles F. Cawley.

Part 3 HEADSTONE LANE

This is another New Line station, opened on 10th. February, 1913. The goods yard on the other side of the bridge at Headstone Lane belonged to Hatch End Station, and was originally known as the Pinner Siding. The yard was closed on and from 14th. November, 1966, and has been replaced by industrial development.

The Royal Train from Glasgow to Euston passing Headstone Lane in 1938 hauled by streamlined LMS 'Princess Coronation' class 4-6-2 No. 6221 Queen Elizabeth. *Until the Second World War the Royal Train was maintained in LNWR livery.*

C.R.L. Coles.

A Down express goods from Camden to Walsall passing Headstone Lane in 1939 headed by ex-LNWR 'Rebuilt Claughton' class 4-6-0 No. 6017 Breadalbane. *The footbridge in the distance on the right connected Harrow View to the fields on the east side of the railway. It was not until 25th. November, 1969, that a road bridge was provided as well, connecting Harrow View to Courtenay Avenue.*

C.R.L. Coles.

LMS Stanier 2-6-4 Tank No. 2589 rushes past Headstone Lane on the Down Fast line with an evening Euston — Tring local train in 1938.

C.R.L. Coles.

One of the two Stanmore Village Branch trains runs empty past Headstone Lane at the end of the evening rush hour en route *for Watford Shed. The locomotive is ex-LMS Stanier 0-4-4 Tank No. 41908, and the date is June, 1952.*

C.R.L. Coles.

N. 177.

London & North Western Railway.

OPENING OF NEW LINE

BETWEEN

Harrow and Wealdstone

AND

- - WATFORD - -

WITH ADDITIONAL STATION AT

HEADSTONE LANE.

Time Table commencing February 10th, 1913, and until further notice.

Euston Station,
London, January 1913.   **FRANK REE**, General Manager.

McCorquodale & Co., Limited, Printers, London—Works, Newton.

Below: *A three-car class '313' unit enters Headstone Lane Station on its journey to Watford Junction in October, 1986. The waiting rooms and toilets at most of the New Line stations are now closed and bricked-up as there are no platform staff to keep an eye on them.*

Ian Brown.

Headstone Lane Station in November, 1930. The booking hall suffered a serious fire in May, 1982, during a period when the station was left unattended. It has since been refurbished but the building externally still looks much the same, except for the removal of the chimney stack. The tobacconist's kiosk, telephone box, and LMS nameboard have also gone, and the "UNDERGROUND" sign has been replaced with a BR 'double arrow'.

London Regional Transport.

The 3.05 p.m. Euston — Rugby train (with two milk tankers) passes the New Line electricity sub-station at Headstone Lane on 13th. July, 1935, hauled by ex-LNWR 'Precursor' class 4-4-0 No. 5301 Emerald. Headstone Lane Station is out of view to the right, on the other side of the road bridge. The coal trucks are standing in Hatch End Goods Yard which was 50 chains south of the passenger station of the same name. Both the goods yard and the electricity sub-station are no longer extant.

Locomotive Club of Great Britain, Ken Nunn collection.

Part 4 HATCH END

This station probably opened on 8th. August, 1842 (see Chapter 1), and was called Pinner, although before opening it had been known as Dove House Bridge. Further name changes occurred on 1st. January, 1897 (Pinner & Hatch End), 1st. February, 1920 (Hatch End for Pinner), and 11th. June, 1956 (Hatch End). The main line platforms were closed on and from 7th. January, 1963.

BR Standard 'Britannia' Pacific 4-6-2 No. 70048 with the Up Emerald Isle *express approaching the Pinner Park Crossing footbridge in April, 1957. This locomotive was subsequently named* The Territorial Army 1908-1958. *The permanent-way staff on the Up Slow line are greasing the fishplates.*

C.R.L. Coles.

Ex-LMS 'Royal Scot' class 4-6-0 No. 46160 Queen Victoria's Rifleman *heads an Up express past the Royal Commercial Travellers' Schools at Hatch End on 5th April, 1957.*

British Rail, London Midland Region.

The Post Office and entrance to Pinner & Hatch End Station before the 1911 rebuilding. This view is from a commercial postcard.

Courtesy Dilwyn Chambers.

Hatch End Station in April, 1933. The board at the entrance reads "LMS HATCH END STATION. DIRECT ELECTRIC TRAINS TO EUSTON, CITY, WEST END AND SOUTH LONDON", while painted on the old Post Office roof the message reads "FREQUENT TRAINS TO WATFORD, CROXLEY GREEN, HARROW, WEMBLEY AND ALL PARTS OF LONDON".

London Regional Transport.

Hatch End Station in October, 1986. Like Harrow & Wealdstone, the canopy over the entrance has been removed giving a clear view of the façade.

Ian Brown.

Gerald Horsley's elaborate festooned garland of fruit, flowers, and foliage (correctly called 'swag') that adorns the front of the station. The rebuilding date and the railway company's initials are also displayed.

C.R.L. Coles

Above: *The Fast lines at Pinner & Hatch End on 24th. March, 1912. The footbridge has been extended on the left to span the New Line, and work is in progress on the platform buildings.*
Courtesy Herfordshire Library Service, Watford Libraries.

Right: *A poster published by the London Electric Railway in 1916 to advertise the LER Bakerloo Line/LNWR New Line route to Pinner & Hatch End. The watercolour is by Nancy Smith and the verse by Robert Bridges, Poet Laureate.*
London Regional Transport.

Hatch End Station, Down New Line platform, in October, 1986. The two doorways are labelled "BICYCLES" and "CLOAK ROOM" in stonework above the lintels. Note Horsley's banded chimney stack, similar to Harrow & Wealdstone.

Ian Brown.

Below: *LNWR advertisement from a brochure advertising "Ye Cocoa Tree, Nowar Hill Park, Pinner" for Band of Hope, Sunday School, and Club Excursions. The brochure noted that the grounds were 1½ miles from the North Western station, but "visitors are rewarded by an exceedingly pretty walk through the country lanes".*

Harrow Local History Collection, London Borough of Harrow.

The east-side entrance to Hatch End Station from The Avenue (between numbers 3 and 5) pictured on 22nd. August, 1956. This entrance and the main line platforms were closed on and from 7th. January, 1963, and the footbridge across the main lines was subsequently removed in readiness for the overhead electrification. However, Platform 3 (Down Fast) remains in position for emergency use.

London Regional Transport.

The main line platforms at Hatch End, circa 1959, viewed from Platform 3. Note the modern style platform buildings which were destined not to last for long. The exit on Platform 6 to The Avenue is signed "WAY OUT TO ROYSTON PARK".

Geoffrey Kichenside.

Above: *An Up express speeds through Hatch End in October, 1986.*

Ian Brown.

Left: *Ex-LNWR 'Prince of Wales' class 4-6-0 No. 5843 on a Down express passing through Hatch End for Pinner in early LMS days.*

Locomotive & General Railway Photographs, courtesy David & Charles.

The Down Midlander *near Hatch End in June, 1953, with ex-LMS 'Jubilee' class 4-6-0 No. 45688* Polyphemus. *This view was taken from the steps of the footbridge connecting Sylvia Avenue with The Avenue.*

C.R.L. Coles.

This Second World War view taken from the farm occupation bridge (now demolished) north of Hatch End shews U.S.A. 'Austerity' class 2-8-0 No. 2415 hauling a Down freight train. Some 400 American locomotives were modified for working on British Railways to help the war effort.

C.R.L. Coles.

North of Hatch End, near the county boundary, ex-LNWR 'Super D' 0-8-0 No.
9352 pilots LMS Stanier 2-8-0 No. 8006 on a Down train of empty coal hoppers
and trucks, while an Up Bakerloo Line train heads for Elephant & Castle. The
date is 21st. March, 1936. The farm occupation bridge mentioned in the previous
view can just be seen on the right.
                Locomotive Club of Great Britain, Ken Nunn collection.

Elegance and speed. Streamlined LMS 'Princess Coronation' class 4-6-2 No. 6221
Queen Elizabeth *with the Down* Coronation Scot *crossing the boundary from*
Middlesex into Hertfordshire in 1938.
                Locomotive Publishing Company, courtesy Ian Allan.

Part 5 THE STANMORE VILLAGE BRANCH

This single-track line was built by the Harrow & Stanmore Railway Company and opened on 18th. December, 1890. The terminus at Stanmore was renamed Stanmore Village on 25th. September, 1950, and was closed to passengers on and from 15th. September, 1952, and to goods on and from 6th. July, 1964. The intermediate station at Belmont opened on 12th. September, 1932, and was closed on and from 5th. October, 1964. A passing loop was in use at Belmont from 1937 until 1952.

Two views of the branch train from Belmont approaching Harrow & Wealdstone. Above, ex-LMS Fowler 2-6-2 Tank No. 40010 with its two-coach push and pull set in August, 1955, and below, a train of British United Traction four-wheel diesel-mechanical cars in June, 1960.

Geoffrey Kichenside.

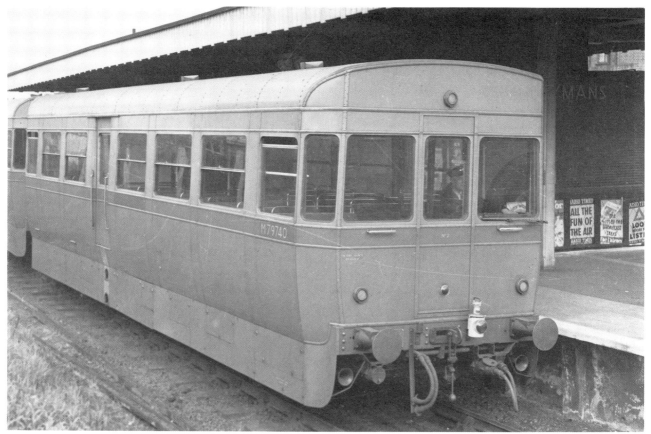

A British United Traction four-wheel set in the west-side loop at Belmont on 24th.
May, 1954. The train is in its original grey, red, and aluminium livery, and has
side-skirts covering the running-gear. These were the first diesel units on the
branch, although the often more reliable steam train continued to make
appearances up to 1962.

British Rail, London Midland Region.

Ex-LNWR 2-4-2 '5ft. 6in. Tank' No. 6711 pushes the 4.55 p.m. Harrow &
Wealdstone — Stanmore train up the 1 in 85 gradient north of Belmont Station on
6th. July, 1948. The branch train was commonly known as the Stanmore Rattler
or, after the closure of Stanmore Village Station, the Belmont Rattler.
Locomotive Club of Great Britain, Ken Nunn collection.

*Ex-LNWR 2-4-2 '4ft. 6in. Tank' No. 6519 leaves Stanmore with the branch train
to Harrow & Wealdstone in 1931. Note that the signals for both directions are
mounted on the same post. The houses on the right are in Wolverton Road,
named after Lord Wolverton, Chairman of the London & Birmingham Railway
and the London & North Western, who lived near-by at Stanmore Park.*
Locomotive Publishing Company, courtesy Ian Allan.

*The rural scene at Stanmore Village Station in July, 1952. Ex-LMS Ivatt 2-6-2
Tank No. 41220 simmers at the head of the branch train.*
Real Photographs Company, courtesy Ian Allan.

A view of Stanmore Station from the buffer stops in LNWR days. The carriage nearest the camera is a control trailer, from where the driver controlled the train when the locomotive was pushing. This method of operation died out with the introduction of diesel multiple units, but is now being revived for main line services as it saves time and resources at termini.

London & North Western Railway Society collection.

A postcard view of Stanmore Station, circa 1910. At the insistence of the Great Stanmore Parish Council, the terminus had to harmonize with its surroundings, so it resembled more a Gothic style church than a railway station. Note the one-horse van, lettered "LONDON & NORTH WESTERN RAILWAY. COLLECTING VAN FOR FAST TRAIN TRAFFIC", and the cab with a rather large load on its roof.

Courtesy Alfred E. Porter.

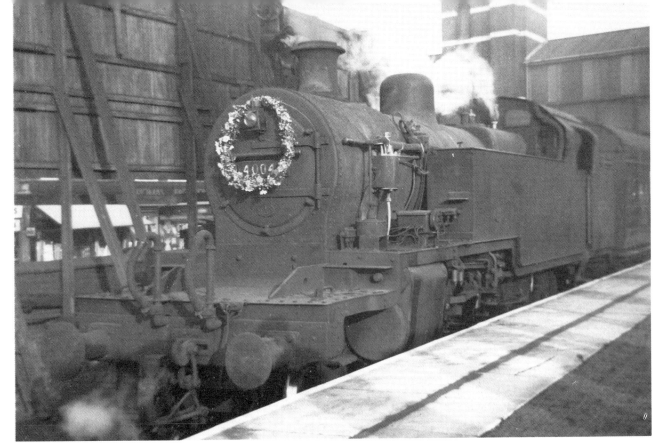

THE LAST TRAINS.
The final Stanmore Rattler *in Platform 7 at Harrow & Wealdstone on Saturday, 13th. September, 1952. The locomotive, ex-LMS Fowler 2-6-2 Tank No. 40043, bears a floral wreath made by Mr. Gordon Foxwell, the porter-signalman at Stanmore Village.*

Geoffrey Kichenside.

The final Belmont Rattler *(Park Royal unit Nos. M50413 and M56169) at Harrow & Wealdstone on Saturday, 3rd. October, 1964, shortly before returning to Watford Shed. The "Axe" wreath was provided by Mrs. Margaret Foxwell, who ran the station bookstall at Belmont.*

John Barnacle.

AFTER CLOSURE.
Desolation at Belmont Station in April, 1966. The track has been lifted, and platform edging is being removed for repairs to platforms on the main line. In July, 1966, the station buildings and footbridge were demolished, and the site is now a car park. The Kenton Lane Bridge is in the background.

Peter G. Scott.

Below: *Stanmore Village Station on 3rd August, 1968. Some of the asbestos cable troughs used in the electrification of the main line still remain on the platform. Despite efforts by local residents to save this picturesque station, it was demolished in July, 1970, except for the frontage on Gordon Avenue which was incorporated (in a much altered form) into the new housing development built on the site. Gordon Avenue is named after Frederick Gordon, founder and Chairman of the Harrow & Stanmore Railway Company.*

Peter G. Scott.

The view looking northwards from the end of the platform at Belmont on 14th. May, 1978, as Harrow Friends of the Earth clear rubbish dumped by very inconsiderate people. This section of trackbed towards the former Wemborough Road — Vernon Drive foot crossing is now administered by the London Wildlife Trust.

Peter G. Scott.

THE END.

From December, 1965, to the end of 1968, the Stanmore Village Branch ended abruptly at these buffer stops near the Christchurch Avenue railway bridge. The embankment here has recently been removed and replaced with an industrial estate, blocking the route of the line and ending any chance of restoring a train service. The access road to the new estate is named Forward Drive, reviving the name of the coffin works that was situated next to the railway and had its own siding. This new industrial development is the last nail in the coffin for the Harrow & Stanmore Railway.

Peter G. Scott.

Bibliography

GENERAL.

Sources of general information include official railway publications, maps, timetables, and minute books of the London & Birmingham Railway Company, the London & North Western Railway Company, the Harrow & Stanmore Railway Company, the London Midland & Scottish Railway Company, British Railways, London Transport, and the Railway Clearing House (mostly from the British Transport Historical Records Collection at the Public Record Office); various Parliamentary Plans (at the Greater London Record Office); the columns of the *Harrow Gazette, Harrow Observer* and the *Harrow Observer & Gazette* (in the Harrow Local History Collection); the *Railway Magazine*; and large scale Ordnance Survey maps (Harrow Local History Collection and the Greater London Record Office).

Other general works include:

Allen, Geoffrey Freeman *The Illustrated History of Railways in Britian* (Marshall Cavendish, 1979).

Borley, H. V. *Chronology of London Railways* (Railway & Canal Historical Society, 1982).

Brine, Tom (Editor) *The Official Guide to the London & North Western Railway* 18th. Edition (Cassell & Co., 1912).

Clinker, C. R. *Clinker's Register of Closed Passenger Stations and Goods Depots in England, Scotland and Wales, 1830-1977* New Edition (Avon-Anglia, 1978).

Dark, Arthur *From Rural Middlesex to London Borough — the growth and development of Harrow illustrated with maps* (London Borough of Harrow, 1981).

★   ★   ★

The following books, contracts, articles, and plans are listed under their respective chapters, although some overlapping inevitably occurs; in the most important cases this is noted. Chapters 1 and 2 are necessarily dealt with together.

Unpublished items followed by "P.R.O." and a reference are located in the Public Record Office at Kew, and the item followed by "G.L.R.O." and a reference is located in the Greater London Record Office at Clerkenwell.

INTRODUCTION.

Dow, George *Railway Heraldry* (David & Charles, 1973).

Ellis, C. Hamilton *The Trains We Loved* (George Allen and Unwin, 1947).

Railway Executive *British Railways Today and Tomorrow* (Railway Executive, 1949).

The Times *London Midland and Scottish Railway Centenary* (reprinted from the "London Midland and Scottish Railway Centenary Number" of *The Times* published on 20th. September, 1938).

CHAPTERS 1 & 2.

Anderson, Roy and Fox, Gregory *A Pictorial Record of LMS Architecture* (Oxford Publishing Co., 1981).

BIBLIOGRAPHY

Architectural Review "Current Architecture — New Stations at Harrow and Pinner" *Architectural Review* September, 1912, pp. 161-165.

Betjeman, John "London Railway Stations" *First and Last Loves* (John Murray, 1952).

Biddle, Gordon and Nock, O. S. (and others) *The Railway Heritage of Britain — 150 Years of Railway Architecture and Engineering* (Michael Joseph, 1983).

Binns & Clifford, Surveyors, Birmingham *Plans of the London & Birmingham Railway London Division* (1840) Corrected and Revised by F. Wood, Rugby (1863) P.R.O. RAIL 384/191.

Bourne, John C. *Drawings of the London & Birmingham Railway with an Historical and Descriptive Account by John Britton* (J. C. Bourne, Ackermann & Co., & C. Tilt, 1839; reproduced by David & Charles, 1970).

British Railways *London on Wheels — Public Transport in London in the Nineteenth Century* (British Railways Board, 1968).

British Railways Press Office *British Railways in Peace and War* (British Railways Press Office, 1944).

Cockburn, J. S. and Baker, T. F. T. (Editors) *The Victoria History of the County of Middlesex, Volume IV* (Oxford University Press, 1971).

Coghlan, Francis *The Iron Road Book and Railway Companion from London to Birmingham, Manchester, and Liverpool* (A. H. Baily & Co., 1838).

Coleman, Terry *The Railway Navvies* (Hutchinson, 1965).

Davies, R. and Grant, M. D. *London and Its Railways* (David & Charles, 1983).

Drake, James *Drake's Road Book of the London and Birmingham and Grand Junction Railways* (Hayward & Moore, 1839).

Ellis, C. Hamilton *Railway History* (Studio Vista, 1966).

Findlay, Sir George *The Working and Management of an English Railway* 6th. Edition (Whittaker & Co., 1899).

Freeling, Arthur *Freeling's Railway Companion from London to Birmingham, Liverpool, and Manchester* New Edition (Tilt & Bogue, no date, *circa* 1841).

Hole, Charles *Life of The Revd. and Ven. William Whitmarsh Phelps, M. A., Volume II* (Hatchards, 1873).

Lloyd, E. *London and Birmingham Railway Guide* (E. Lloyd, 1838).

London & Birmingham Railway Company *Contract No. II (Harrow)* (1834) P.R.O. RAIL 384/163.

London & Birmingham Railway Company *Harrow Weald Station Contract* (1837) P.R.O. RAIL 384/177.

BIBLIOGRAPHY

London & North Western Railway Company *Euston to Watford Additional Lines, Widening between Harrow and Bushey and new railways between Bushey and the Rickmansworth Branch (Contract No.3)* (1910) P.R.O. RAIL 410/952.

London & North Western Railway Company *Free House Passes to and from Euston Station* (1854) P.R.O. RAIL 410/1242.

London & North Western Railway Company *Harrow & Wealdstone Station Contract* (1910) P.R.O. RAIL 410/953.

London Midland & Scottish Railway Company *A Century of Progress, London — Birmingham 1838-1938* (LMS, 1938).

May, Trevor F. "Harrow School and the London & Birmingham Railway" from *A Study of Harrow School in its Relationship to its Neighbourhood Throughout the 19th. Century* (1969) Unpublished MS.

Mowat, C. L. "The Heyday of the British Railway System: Vanishing Evidence and the Historian's Task" *The Journal of Transport History* New Series Volume 1 No.1, February, 1971, pp. 1-17 (Leicester University Press).

Osborne, Edward Cornelius and Osborne, W. *Osborne's London & Birmingham Railway Guide* (E. C. & W. Osborne, 1840).

Pinner & Hatch End W.E.A. Local History Group *Harrow Before Your Time* (Pinner & Hatch End W.E.A., 1972).

Pugh, Derek G. "Runaway Through Harrow" (Herbert Spencer) *Railway Magazine* Volume 130 No.1000, August, 1984, p.306.

Railway Gazette "LMS Centenary of Opening of First Main-Line Railway" Supplement to the *Railway Gazette* (16th. September, 1938; also re-published by Oxford Publishing Co., 1975).

Roscoe, Thomas (assisted by Lecount, Peter) *The London and Birmingham Railway* (Charles Tilt and Wrightson & Webb, 1839).

Roxeth Research Group *Roxeth Remembered* (London Borough of Harrow, 1984).

Scott, Peter G. *The Harrow & Stanmore Railway* 2nd. Edition (Hartest Productions, 1981).

Spencer, Herbert *An Autobiography, Volume 1* (Williams & Norgate, 1904).

Thomas, Joseph *Railroad Guide, from London to Birmingham* (Joseph Thomas, 1839).

Tootell, J. *Valuation of the Parish of Harrow in the County of Middlesex made for the purpose of the Parochial Assessment* (1852) G.L.R.O. Acc. 590/2 (map), Acc. 590/4 (register).

Torre, Revd. H. J. *Recollections of Schooldays at Harrow more than Fifty Years Ago* edited by the Hon. and Revd. George T.O. Bridgeman (Charles Simms & Co., 1890).

BIBLIOGRAPHY

White, H. P. *A Regional History of the Railways of Great Britain, Volume 3, Greater London* (Phoenix House, 1963; and David & Charles, 1970).

Wilkins, Harry *Greenhill* (London Borough of Harrow, 1981).

Wilkins, Harry *Looking Back... The Wealdstone Scene* (H. M. Wilkins, 1976).

CHAPTER 3.

Johnson, Peter *The British Travelling Post Office* (Ian Allan, 1985).

SEE ALSO: Allen, Cecil J. *Famous Trains* [CHAPTER 6] and Railway Gazette "LMS Centenary..." [CHAPTERS 1 & 2].

CHAPTER 4.

Cummings, John *Railway Motor Buses and Bus Services in the British Isles, 1902-1933, Volume 1* (Oxford Publishing Co., 1978).

May, Trevor F. "Road Passenger Transport in Harrow in the Nineteenth and Early Twentieth Centuries" *The Journal of Transport History* New Series Volume 1 No.1, February, 1971, pp. 18-38 (Leicester University Press).

CHAPTER 5.

Atkinson, F. G. B. and Adams, B. W. *London's North Western Electric — A Jubilee History* (Eltrac Publications for the Electric Railway Society, 1962).

Daily Graphic "Railways Moving with the Times.." *Daily Graphic* 3rd. June, 1912, p.13.

Hardy, Brian, Frew, Iain D. O. and Willson, Ross *A Chronology of the Electric Railways of Great Britain and Ireland* (Eltrac Publications for the Electric Railway Society, 1981).

Lee, Charles E. *Sixty Years of the Bakerloo* (London Transport, 1966).

Talbot, Edward, Dow, George, Millard, Philip and Davis, Peter *LNWR Liveries* (Historical Model Railway Society, 1985).

SEE ALSO: White H. P. *A Regional History...* [CHAPTERS 1 & 2].

CHAPTER 6.

Allen, Cecil J. *Famous Trains* (Meccano Limited, 1928).

British Railways *Euston Station, A Brief Historical Sketch* (pamphlet, British Railways, 1957).

British Railways *The Royal Scot Golden Jubilee, 1927-1977* (table card, British Railways, 1977).

Caplan, Neil *Titled Trains: 1; 'Royal Scot'* (Ian Allan, 1986).

CHAPTER 7.

Earl, Driver L. A. (in collaboration with Greenleaf, H. N.) *Speeding North*

BIBLIOGRAPHY

with the 'Royal Scot' — A Day in the Life of a Locomotive Man (Oxford University Press, 1939).

Vale, Edmund (with pen and ink sketches by Glazebrook, F. H. and Hutchings, R. M.) *LMS Route Book No.2 — Liverpool to London (Euston), Along the Viking Border* (LMS, no date).

CHAPTER 8.

Anon. " 'Snatch': A Railway Story" *The New Penny Magazine* Volume II, 1899, pp. 338-340.

Coombs, L. F. E. *The Harrow Railway Disaster 1952 — Twenty-five Years On* (David & Charles, 1977).

Holt, G. O. "An Early Railway Accident at Harrow" *Journal of the Railway and Canal Historical Society* May, 1958, pp. 47-49.

Ministry of Transport *Report on the Double Collision which occurred on 8th. October, 1952, at Harrow & Wealdstone Station in the London Midland Region British Railways* (H.M.S.O., 1953).

Neele, George P. *Railway Reminiscences* (McCorquodale, 1904, and E.P. Publishing, 1974).

Rolt, L. T. C. *Red for Danger* (John Lane, The Bodley Head, 1955; and David & Charles, 1971).

CHAPTER 9.

Bonham-Carter, J. (Chief Operating Officer, British Railways Board) "The London Midland Electrification" *Railway Students' Bulletin* No.3, April, 1966, p.2ff. (Railway Students' Association).

British Railways *Rail Week — Harrow* (programme for Harrow Rail Week, British Railways, 1966).

British Transport Commission *All Along the Line* (British Transport Commission, 1959).

Semmens, P. W. B. "Locomotive Practice and Performance — 1984 Electric Records" *Railway Magazine* Volume 131 No.1008, April, 1985, pp. 173-177.

Smithson, Alison and Peter *The Euston Arch and the Growth of the London, Midland & Scottish Railway* (Thames & Hudson, 1968).

SEE ALSO: Hardy, Frew and Willson *A Chronology of the Electric Railways...* [CHAPTER 5].

CHAPTER 10.

Coles, C. R. L. *Railways Through the Chilterns* (Ian Allan, 1980).

Talbot, Edward *LNWR Miscellany* (Oxford Publishing Co., 1978).

Talbot, Edward *LNWR Miscellany Volume 2* (Oxford Publishing Co., 1980).

SEE ALSO: Scott, Peter G. *The Harrow & Stanmore Railway* [CHAPTERS 1 & 2].

INDEX

Railway stations, signal boxes, tunnels and bridges are (in general) indexed under their present names, with a note on former names in parenthesis.

Figures in *italic* type refer to illustrations, or captions to illustrations, and an asterisk (*) denotes that the reference is to a footnote.

INDEX

INDEX

INDEX

INDEX

conversion to 3rd. rail operation, 72.
electric multiple units,
    Bakerloo Line, *69*, 72, *74*, *95*, *120*, *141*.
    BR Standard, 72, *73*, *110*.
    class '313', 72, 74, *131*.
    1st. class withdrawn, 72.
    G.E.C., 71, 72.
    headcodes, *73*.
    Joint Stock, 69, 70, *70*.
    Oerlikon, 70 – 72, *71*, *121*.
    seven-car trains, 71, 72.
    Siemens, 70.
electrification, 50, 65, 69, 70, *114*,
    generating station, 85.
    line voltage increased, 72.
    sub-stations, *107*, *132*.
'Euston to Watford Additional Lines' contract, 44, 46.
Harrow & Wealdstone accident (1952), 93, 94, *95 – 97*.
opening (in stages), 48, 65, 69, 70.
overcrowding, 70, 72.
publicity poster, *136*.
run-down of services, 72, 74.
signalling, 46, *50*, *51*, 71, 72, *125*.
station design, *112*.
steam service, 65, 68 – 70.
timetables, *53*, 65, *67*, 68, *68*, 72, *131*.
New Penny Magazine, 90,
    (quoted), 89.
New York World's Fair, *77*.
North Union Railway, 56.
North Wembley Signal Box, 93.
North Wembley Station, 48, *83*, 85, 102.
North-Western Country Homes, 68, *68*.
North Western Electric network, 65, 69, 72.
Northern Line, 74,
    SEE ALSO 'Edgware & Hampstead Railway'.
Northolt, wireless station, 85.
Northwick, Lord, 14, 17, 40.
Northwick Avenue footbridge, *76*, *108*, *109*.
Northwick Park, 106.
Nowell, Joseph, and Sons, 15*ff*,
    completion of contract, 24.

O

Omnibus services,
    'Country Coach Proprietors', 61.
    LNWR, 50, 61, 62,
        Harrow Station routes, 42, *60*, 61, 62, *63*, *64*.
        Pinner Station route, *60*, 62.
        'Road Motor Car' ticket, *62*.
        staff *5*.
    London General Omnibus Company 62.
    LT,
        in competition with Stanmore Village Branch, 50.
        route 136, 62.
        route 230, *127*.
    privately operated, 61.
    SEE ALSO 'Road Coach services'.
Oxford, 13.
Oxhey Lane, farm occupation bridge, *140*, *141*.
Oxhey Lane Bridge *(now Little Oxhey Lane)*, 17.
Oxhey Lane Cutting, 17, *17*, 24.
Oxhey Lane Tunnel, 13, 17.
Oystermouth Railway, 8, 9.

P

Paddington Canal, 20.
Paddington Station, 20, 94.
Paines Lane, 62.
Palmerston, Lord 84.
Parliamentary tickets, *12*.
Pearson, Mr., 32.
Peel, Sir Robert, 84.
Phelps, Reverend William Whitmarsh, 32.
Piccadilly Line, 70.
Pinner, 27, 35,
    Cocoa Tree [Tavern], 62, *137*.
    omnibus services, *60*, 61, 62.
Pinner (in Harrow), Parish of, *Frontispiece*, 16, 17, 27.
Pinner Drive, *35*, 37.
Pinner Gates — SEE 'Pinner Park Crossing'.
Pinner Green, 27, 62.
Pinner Park Crossing, 17, *18/19*, 27, *81*, *133*,
    closed, 40.
Pinner Park Estate, 16, 17.
Pinner Road, 62.
Pinner Siding, *18/19*, 129.
Pinner Station (Metropolitan), 62.
Pinner View, 37*.
Plans — SEE 'Maps and plans.
Pompeii, 'rutways' in, 20.
Port, Thomas, 84.
Postal services — SEE 'Royal Mail' and 'Travelling Post Offices'.
Preston, 72.
Priest, John, 17.
Primrose Hill Tunnel, *25*, 37, 40, *83*, 85, 86.
Prisoners of war, 72.
Push and pull working, 48, 68, *145*.

Q

Quainton, 13.
Queen Elizabeth, 75.
Queen Mary, 65.
Queen's Arms public house, 29, *31*, 32, 37, 89, *119*.
Queen's Park Station *(previously suffixed '(West Kilburn)')*, 65, 69, 86.
Quintinshill, Gretna, 94.

R

R101 airship, *113*.
Railway Guides,
    Bradshaw's, 28, 81.
    Coghlan's Iron Road Book, Frontispiece.
    Lloyd's London & Birmingham, *24 – 26*, 26.
    LMS Route Book No.2, 6, 81, *82/83*,
        (quoted), 85, 86.
    Official Guide to the London & North Western, 48, 81,
        (quoted), 61, 65, 81.
    Osborne's London & Birmingham, Front cover,
        (quoted), 26.
    Roscoe's London & Birmingham, *23*.
Railway Heritage of Britain, The, 28.
Railway Hotel, Wealdstone, 32, *32*.
'Railway mania', 7.
Rainhill Locomotive Trials, 8.
Ramsay, John, 55.
Red Cross, International, *111*.
Refreshment stops, *28*.
Regent's Canal, 13, 15, 23.

Regent's Park, 7.
Rennie, Sir John, 13.
Reshaping of British Railways, The, 7.
Richmond Station, 65.
Rickmansworth, 13.
Rickmansworth Branch, *67*, 70.
Ridgeway, The, footbridge, *76*, *108*, *109*.
Road coach services,
    Denbigh Hall-Rugby, 25, *26*, 27.
    Harrow-London, 7.
Road transport, development of, 48.
Rocket, 8.
Rolinson, Station Master C. S., 94.
Roman wagon wheels, gauge of, 20.
Roman Wall, 26.
Roxborough Bridge, 40, 62.
Roxeth, *36*, 42, 61, 62, *128*.
Roxeth Corner, 62.
Royal Commercial Travellers' Schools, 16, *133*.
Royal Mail *43, 46, 60, 62*,
    SEE ALSO 'Travelling Post Offices' and 'Mail Exchange Apparatus'.
Royal Train, *129*.
Royston Park, *138*.
Rugby, 25, 55.
Rugby Power Signal Box, 102.
Ruislip, 27.

S

Saint John Ambulance Association, *92*.
Saint Pancras Parish, 15.
Saint Pancras Station, 94.
Saint Thomas's Hospital, 16, 17, *18/19*.
Salvation Army, 37, 94.
Sandridge Close — SEE 'Marlborough Road'.
Scotland, 40, 75.
Scott, Sir Gilbert, 84.
Second World War, 7, 48, 70, 72, 75, *109*, *129*, *140*.
Shaw, Richard Norman, 44.
Sheepcote Lane *(now Watford Road)*, 106, *108*.
Shelvey, Driver "Duke", 90, 91, *91*.
Signalling *50, 90*, 91 – 94, 101, 102, *115*, *125*, *126*, *144*,
    Automatic Warning System, 94, 101.
    fog, 34, 90 – 92.
    permissive block, 89, 90.
    SEE ALSO names of individual signal boxes.
Simpson, Driver, 89, 90.
Smith, C. J., *22*, 30, *33*.
Smith, Nancy, *136*.
"Snatch", 90, 91, *91*.
South Harrow Station, 62.
South Kenton Station, 72, *77*.
South Mimms, 13.
Southam, 13.
Southern Railway, 10, *107*.
Speeding North with the 'Royal Scot' (quoted), 85 – 88.
Spencer, Herbert, 32, 34.
Spiers, Wallace, *113*.
Stage coaches — SEE 'Road coach services'.
Stanmore — SEE 'Great Stanmore' or 'Little Stanmore.
Stanmore Branch *(originally Metropolitan Railway, then L.T. Bakerloo Line, and now Jubilee Line)*, 50.
Stanmore Marsh, 40.
Stanmore Park, 9, *144*.

158

INDEX

The Author.

Peter Scott has always lived within a mile or so of Harrow & Wealdstone Station. His early interest in railways was stimulated by visits to the Euston Main Line at Kenton Recreation Ground, the Stanmore Village Branch, and West Hampstead Midland Station (where his uncle worked). He later helped to organize trips with the famous Flying Scotsman *locomotive, and has also tried his hand at firing and driving steam locomotives. His professional career has been spent with the London Electricity Board (looking down holes in the road!), and he is also Director and Secretary of Greenhill Estate Limited. Since 1983 he has looked after the bells at Great Stanmore Parish Church, following in the footsteps of another local historian, the late Edward Leversuch. His present local history interest is in railways and place-names, and his previous publications include* The Harrow & Stanmore Railway *and* Vestry Arc — The Historic Public Lighting Columns of Saint Pancras.

Cover illustrations (from top to bottom):
Front: *LNWR 'Precedent' class 2-4-0 No. 2182* Giraffe *passes through Harrow & Wealdstone with an Up express in 1899.*
    Locomotive & General Railway Photographs, courtesy David & Charles.

Part of a London & Birmingham Railway train from an illustration in Osborne's London & Birmingham Railway Guide *(1840). The locomotive is an Edward Bury 2-2-0 No. 34.*
    Courtesy Railway Gazette.

Back: *Illustration of a 25kV a.c. electric locomotive, as used on BR publicity in 1966.*
    Peter G. Scott's collection,
    reproduced courtesy British Rail, London Midland Region.

LMS 'Jubilee' class 4-6-0 No. 5741 Leinster *makes plenty of smoke as it heads a Down Birmingham express past the mail pick-up standards south of Harrow & Wealdstone in 1947.*
    Locomotive Publishing Company, courtesy Ian Allan.

An LNWR 'Super D' 0-8-0 hauls "A. WOOSTER & SONS" coal trucks on this enlargement of their 1920's billhead illustration.
    Courtesy A. Wooster & Sons.